วัดหลวงพ่อสดธรรมกายาราม

อ.ดำเนินสะดวก จ.ราชบุรี

Sunday Dhamma Talks

Volume 2

by

Dr. Phra Rajyanvisith

Interviews on the

National Broadcasting System

of Thailand

January - June BE 2551 (2008)

Published by

Wat Luang Phor Sodh Dhammakāyārām

Damnoen Saduak District, Rajburi Province

70130, Thailand

Recognized Excellence

- Rajburi: Provincial Meditation Institute & Provincial Pali Studies Center;
- Sangha Ecclesiastical Region 15 Academic Services Unit for Mahachulalongkornrajavidyalaya University (Covering four central provinces)
- National Coordination Center of Provincial Meditation Institutes of Thailand
- Wat Luang Phor Sodh Buddhist Meditation Institute, Associated Institution of the World Buddhist University

1st Edition May 2009

ISBN 978-974-94626-4-5

CONTENTS

Appendices

We dedicate this book and any merit it may generate, along with all our efforts at Wat Luang Phor Sodh - The beautiful campus, the Abbot's teachings, Phra Mahā Jetiya Somdej, the International Retreats, the Thai Retreats, and the 24-hour Meditation Vihara - to our beloved

Venerable Chao Khun

Phra Mongkol-Thepmuni

Luang Phor Sodh Candasaro

Acknowledgements

I am deeply indebted to the National Broadcasting System of Thailand for making these Sunday Dhamma Talks possible. May their valiant efforts continue to prosper with the efficacy of the merit accumulated from this Dhamma propagation.

I would also like to take this opportunity to thank Phra Khru Baitika Dr. Barton Yanathiro for serving as interviewer during these broadcasts and as the editor of this volume. May he also share in reaping the benefits of any merit generated.

Finally, let me also express my deep gratitude to Phra Mahā Prasert Paññāseṭṭho and Phra Natpakanan Guṇaṅkaro of the Wat Luang Phor Sodh Publication's Office and to Phra Mahā Somchat and the Wat Luang Phor Sodh Audio-Visual Staff, as well as to my faithful Secretary Phra Mahā Chainipoj for their indispensable support in making this endeavor successful.

Phra Rajyanvisith

Dr. Phra Rajyanvisith
Abbot, Wat Luang Phor Sodh

Dr. Phra Rajyanvisith (Interviewee)
Abbot, Wat Luang Phor Sodh

Phra Khru Baitika Dr. Barton Yanathiro
Interviewer and Editor

Chapter I
Introduction

Hello. I'm Phra Bart - Phra Khru Baitika Dr. Barton Yanathiro - from the United States. In BE 2550 (CE 2007) the National Broadcasting System of Thailand invited Venerable Chao Khun Dr. Phra Rajyanvisith to initiate a series of Sunday Dhamma Talks in English on the first Sunday of each month. I served as the interviewer in the broadcasts and am the editor of this volume.

This is the second issue in a continuing series. Dr. Phra Rajyanvisith has an extremely impressive record, now well recognized from local through international levels. You will find that the broadcasts compiled here go far beyond the ordinary in both scholastic erudition and inspiration for meditation practice.

Volume One presented the first six months, July to December 2007. It began with an overview of Lord Buddha's teachings, and continued through the first of the three Higher Trainings *(Adhisikkhā)* which covers "*Sīla*" or Moral Behavior.

Volume Two

Volume Two covers the second six months, January to June 2008. It begins by completing coverage of the Three Higher Trainings. Chapters two and three present the Second Higher Training on Concentration Meditation *(Samādhi)* which purifies the mind from the engulfing Five Hindrances (*Nivaraṇa*) by successive concentration through four *Jhānas* or states of internal absorption. *Samadha* Meditation, which Lord Buddha learned from his teachers, provides the preparation and tools for effective *Vipassanā* Insight Meditation, which was Lord Buddha's added discovery. Chapter four completes the Higher Trainings with the Training on transcendental Wisdom *(Paññā)*, which is achieved through *Vipassanā* Meditation.

How to Meditate

The text then turns to its primary focus on Lord Buddha's fundamental teachings on how to meditate, as presented in The "Greater Discourse on the Four Foundations of Mindfulness" (*Mahā Satipaṭṭhāna Sutta* in the *Dīgha Nikāya*). Venerable Dr. Phra Raj-yanvisith's careful attention to accurate translation from the original Pali plus his own extensive experience as a meditation master combine to rescue Lord Buddha's teachings from a handful of misinterpretations that are currently widespread and threatening to mislead both students of scripture and meditation practitioners.

For example, the currently popular translation of "*Kāye kāyānupassī Viharati*" as "contemplating the body as body" misinterprets and obscures the original "body-in-the-body" which thousands of meditatiors have now seen themselves. Such key revelations are found throughout the broadcasts, and highlighted in the Summary and Conclusion Chapter.

Each broadcast also includes a brief meditation experience, encouraging the listener to "See for himself." Thus, this volume both elucidates and encourages practice of Lord Buddha's most fundamental teachings on meditation. You will be surprised to learn how deep inside meditation can draw the mind. Learn how astounding and wonderful it can be.

Dr. Phra Rajyanvisith

Now, I would like to introduce Venerable Dr. Phra Rajyanvisith for those who are not yet familiar with him. He is the Abbot of Wat Luang Phor Sodh *Dhammakāyārām* in Damnoen Saduak District of Rajburi Province, and one of Thailand's most eminent Meditation Masters and Buddhist Scholars. He has been broadcasting, lecturing, and publishing about Buddhism in Thai since 1970 (BE 2513), and toured universities in the United States for four years, before the press of responsibilities at home became too demanding.

Dr. Phra Rajyanvisith's mission is to revitalize Buddhism, placing equal emphasis on academic study and meditation practice. In 1986, he ordained as a monk with the name Sermchai Jayamanggalo. In 1998, he received the Royal Ecclesiastical Rank of Phra Bhavana Visutthikhun; and in 2004 he was awarded the rank of Phra Rajyanvisith. He has published over 70 books, 400 articles, and two journals, and recorded over 1,000 Dhamma lectures. In BE 2550 (CE 2007), he was awarded an honorary doctorate in Buddhist Administration from Mahachulalongkornrajavidyalaya University. In 2008, he became President of the Executive Committee of the National Coordination Center of Provincial Meditation Institutes of Thailand (Elected by the Directors of Provincial Meditation Institutes from throughout the country at a Seminar and Practicum organized by the National Buddhist Office 23-25 April 2008 at Wat Yanawa, Bangkok, Thailand, and recognized by the Sangha Body).

Wat Luang Phor Sodh

Dr. Phra Rajyanvisith has led Wat Luang Phor Sodh to become a recognized center of excellence in meditation practice, Pali language, scripture studies, and temple administration. The temple conducts or coordinates training locally for Rajburi Province, regionally for Ecclesiastical Region 15 (four central provinces), nationally for the Thai National Office of Buddhism, and internationally for the World Buddhist University.

At the provincial level, Wat Luang Phor Sodh is one of very few temples in Thailand designated as both a Provincial Pali Studies Center (since 1999) and a Provincial Meditation Institute (since 2000).

At the regional level, Wat Luang Phor Sodh serves as an Academic Services Unit for Mahachulalongkornrajavidyalaya University, training monks from throughout Ecclesiastical Region 15, which consists of four central provinces: Samut Song Khram, Ratchaburi, Petchaburi, and Prachuapkhirikhan. The Wat currently provides pre-university courses for monks lacking prerequisites, and a Bachelor's Degree Program in Buddhist Studies, and a Master's Degree Program in Buddhist Administration.

At the national level, Wat Luang Phor Sodh has served as the Coordination Center for all Provincial Meditation Institutes throughout Thailand since 2008.

Also, in collaboration with the National Office of Buddhism, the temple has trained over 1,500 senior Thai monks from throughout the country to become teachers of *Vipassanā* Meditation. In addition, Venerable Dr. Phra Rajyanvisith's perceptive *Dhamma* lectures are broadcast regularly over the National Broadcasting System of Thailand, on both radio and TV, in both Thai and English.

At the international level, the Wat Luang Phor Sodh Buddhist Meditation Institute (BMI) has been recognized as an Associated Institution of the World Buddhist University since 2006. It trains a continual stream of international meditators in English, with exceptional results. In 2007, Four out of seven participants (57%) meditated to *Jhāna*, seeing their refined human body. Four out of ten (42%) transcended in meditation to *Dhammakāya*; and, three out of ten (29%) meditated to experiencing Nirvāṇa *(Nibbāna)* temporarily.

Meditators are enthusiastic:

- A once in a lifetime opportunity!
- Showed me a new world!
- Put life in a much bigger perspective!
- Encouraged me to live in a more altruistic way!

• In Nirvana I was overwhelmed; I knew I don't have to doubt any more!"

But, the number served is still small. BMI is initiating "Meditation Online" at www.meditationpark.org to reach more meditators.

Conclusion

In conclusion, Dr. Phra Rajyanvisith and Wat Luang Phor Sodh have an extremely impressive record which has now been well recognized from provincial through international levels. This is an extremely unique blend of academic and transcendental knowledge, rarely available in English. Please take full advantage of it.

Phra Khru Baitika Dr. Barton Yanathiro
Interviewer and Editor

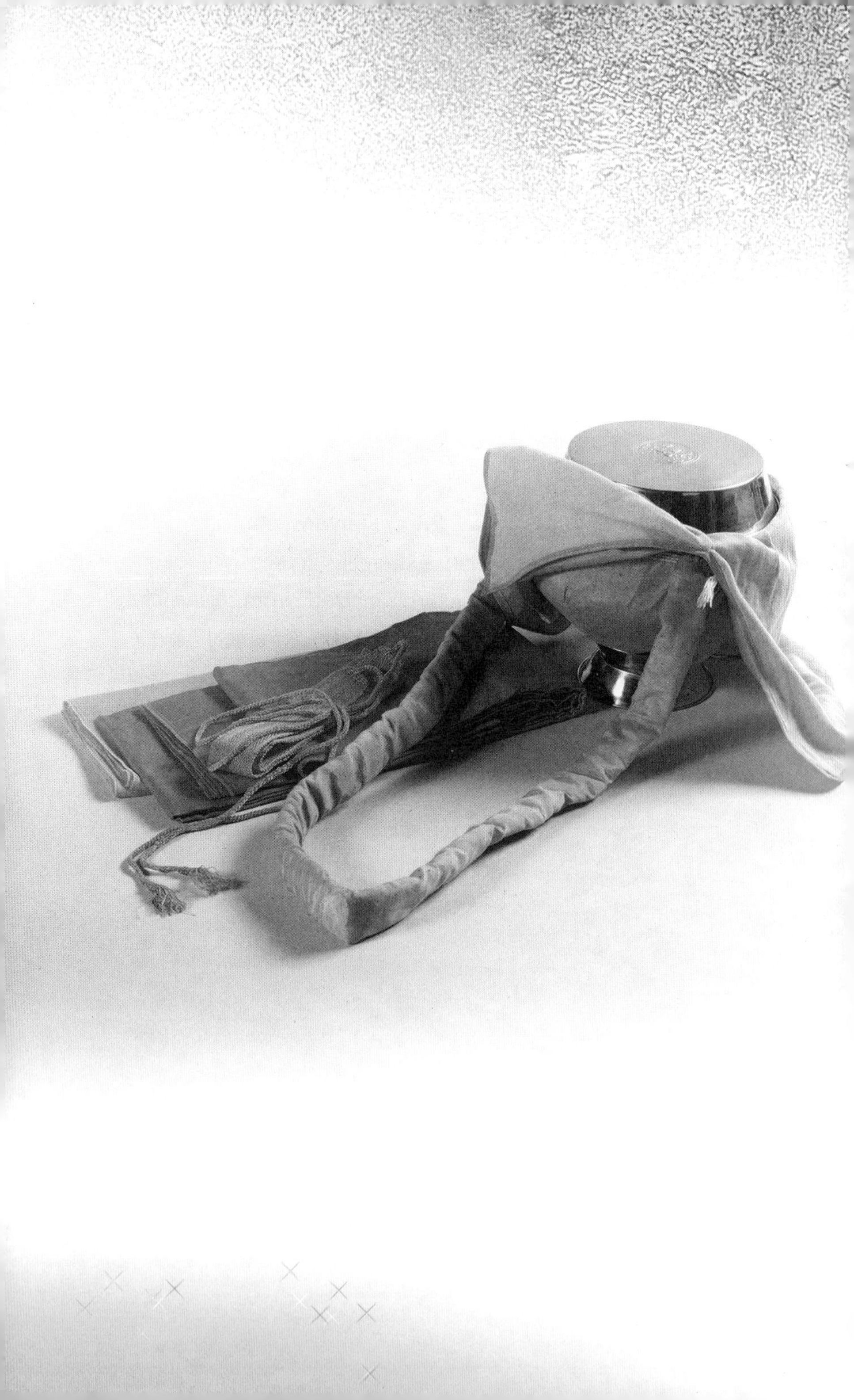

Chapter 2

Samādhi or Concentration:

The Second Training

06 January 2008

Question 1: Welcome, Dr. Phra Rajyanvisith. This is our seventh Sunday Dhamma Talk, and, now, we have a whole new year ahead. We were in the midst of reflecting on the three trainings - (1) *Adhisīla-sikkhā* - training in higher morality, meaning *Sīla* or moral behavior, (2) *Adhicittā-sikkhā* - training in higher mentality, meaning *Samādhi* or Concentration Meditation, and (3) *Adhipaññāsikkhā* - training in higher wisdom, meaning *Vipassanā* or Insight Meditation to develop Right Wisdom. These three trainings summarize the Noble Eightfold Path.

Today, we will consider the second training - *Samādhi* or Concentration Meditation. First, however, since this is a new year, please summarize briefly what we discussed last time regarding *Sīla* or moral behavior.

Answer 1: Happy New Year, ladies and gentlemen. *Sīla* or moral behavior constitutes the necessary foundation for progress in meditation. All religions teach us to avoid evil and do good. Lord Buddha added: "And purify your own mind." A pure mind sustains avoiding evil actions and doing good. But, more importantly, purifying the mind is the pathway to higher levels of consciousness, transcendence, and enlightenment. Thus, it not only supports social harmony, but also leads to personal mental development.

The crux of *Sīla* or moral behavior is following the Five Precepts. These are not commandments, but trainings based on Lord Buddha's enlightened insight into the natural law governing rebirth. They provide the key to avoiding rebirth in Hell. The first is to avoid killing living beings - not just human beings, but all creatures. The second is to avoid stealing, cheating and corruption. The third precept is to avoid sexual misconduct such as adultery. Fourth is to avoid false, divisive and indecent speech, including not only lying, but also backbiting, coarse language, and gossip. Finally, the Fifth Precept is to avoid intoxicants, including both alcohol and drugs.

Lord Buddha developed great compassion for all human beings, because he saw that the large majority will be reborn into the suffering worlds as animals, demons, hungry ghosts, or hell-beings. The immediate cause of this is following uncontrolled cravings or passions. The root cause is ignorance - for example, not knowing the past; not knowing the future; not knowing the cause and effect linking the past, the present and the future; not knowing dependent origination or the cause of the cause of the cause and the root cause of suffering; and finally, not knowing the Four Noble Truths. In brief, not knowing what is right and wrong, not knowing the Law of Karma, and not knowing the horrible future consequences of doing evil. There is no forgiveness; no way out. No one else can help. It is just a natural law - do good, get good; do evil, get evil. The only solution is good personal behavior and constant vigilance to avoid evil.

Question 2 : Now, let us turn to *Samādhi*. What is the purpose of *Samādhi* Meditation? What should we expect to achieve from it?

Answer 2 : *Samādhi* is Concentration Meditation. It combines developing inner peace and concentration together. For most new meditators in today's hectic world, the immediate objective is to cope with stress and develop personal serenity. *Samādhi* provides this immediately. But, the Buddhist objective is higher. It is raising consciousness to more refined planes through purifying the mind.

Direct benefits that can be anticipated include improved mental and physical health and enhanced concentration. The meditator develops distancing from the passions, cravings and delusional attachments which spin us around in circles. This results in a more peacefully happy life and indirectly fosters harmony in the family, the society, and the world.

Beyond these external consequences, *Samādhi* Meditation develops the mental tools for effective, objective observation of nature for use in *Vipassanā* Insight Meditation to develop Right Wisdom. In *Vipassanā*, the meditator becomes able to penetrate the Four Noble Truths to see clearly and compare objectively the compound, impermanent, unsatisfactory suffering, and hollow emptiness of this world with the non-compound, eternal, peacefully happy, and ultimately meaningful essence of *Nibbāna*.

Question 3 : Thank you, Venerable Sir. Now, please tell us more about what *Samādhi* is - what should we contemplate and what should we do.

Answer 3 : Most broadly, *Samādhi* or *Adhi-cittasikkhā* is higher mental training. Lord Buddha listed nine effective subjects for *Samādhi* or Concentration Meditation. The first four are the key Foundations of

Mindfulness - the body, feelings, mind and mental objects. We shall review each of these in detail. The next three are contemplation of old age, sickness, and death. Eighth is meditation that we are all ultimately destined to be separated from what we love, even from our own self. Finally, the ninth theme is that we are all inevitably subject to reap the karmic consequences of our own actions. This is a natural law of cause and effect. There is no way out. Only conscientious good behavior can save us.

Samādhi covers three of the eight factors of the Noble Eightfold Path: (1) Right Effort, *Sammā-vāyāma;* (2) Right Mindfulness, *Sammāsati;* and (3) Right Concentration, *Sammāsamādhi.*

The first factor, Right Effort, is defined as four exertions:

The first effort is to prevent the arising of new bad habits, that is, bad actions, speech or thought. Examples of bad actions are intentionally killing living beings, stealing or cheating, sexual misconduct, wrong livelihood, addiction to intoxicants, gambling, and excessive hedonism. Examples of bad speech are lying, back-biting, coarse language and gossiping. Examples of bad thoughts include evil intentions, greed, lust, hot temperedness, hatred, and deluded thinking or holding erroneous beliefs.

The second effort is the exertion to abandon bad habits, such as these, which have already arisen.

The third effort is to develop new good habits, that is good actions, speech, and thoughts. Good actions are the opposites of bad actions. For example, treating other beings with sympathy and mercy, generous benevolence, loyalty to one's spouse, right occupation, clear-headed concentration, and alert awareness of what is good and bad.

The fourth effort is to maintain good habits which have already arisen, such as those just mentioned.

The second factor of the Eightfold Path, Right Mindfulness, is defined as the Four Foundations of Mindfulness: successive inner perception *(anupassanā)* and contemplation of body, feelings, mentality, and *dhamma*. The Greater Discourse on the Foundations of Mindfulness (the *Mahāsatipaṭṭhāna Sutta* in the Digha Nikāya) is Lord Buddha's main sermon on meditation.

It lists six methods for mindfulness of the body: Mindfulness of breathing, posture, and actions; Contemplation of body parts as repulsive and as just elements - water, earth, fire or wind; and, nine meditations on corpses, considering that this body too, will become like that. The meditator continues contemplating the body-in-the-body both internally and externally along with the arising and vanishing of phenomena in the body. He remains detached, being aware that there is body, without any clinging.

Similarly, the meditator perceives and contemplates the feelings-in-the-feelings as pleasant, painful or neutral, without any clinging.

Then, the meditator perceives and contemplates the mind-in-the-mind as lustful, hateful, deluded, distracted, developed, unsurpassed, concentrated, liberated, or the opposites of these states, without any clinging.

Finally, the meditator perceives and contemplates the *dhammā*-in-the-*dhammā*, specifically: (1) the Five Hindrances; (2) the Five Aggregates; (3) the Six Sense Organs and their sense-objects; (4) the Seven Factors of Enlightenment; and (5) the Four Noble Truths. Lord Buddha concludes, the Four Foundations of Mindfulness are the one way street to the purification of beings for overcoming sorrow and distress and gaining the right path for the realization of *Nibbāna.*

Finally, mental training also covers Right Concentration or *Sammāsamādhi. Samādhi* is defined as developing the Four *Rūpa Jhānas* or States of Absorption, going deeper and deeper inside to purify the mind from the Five Hindrances, which obscure clear-sightedness, to transform the normal human senses into powerful instruments of observation, enabling the necessary and sufficient, reliable and valid collection of the relevant data required for direct, lucid comprehension of the true nature of reality. Prince Siddhattha intuitively meditated to the First *Jhāna* when he was only seven years old. Later, when he recognized the futility of seeking enlightenment through self-torture, this memory led him onto the correct path.

Question 4 : Now, please tell us about the Four *Jhānas* or States of Absorption.

Answer 4 : The normal human mind is blurred by Five Hindrances. The Five Hindrances, are Sleepines or Laziness *(Thīna-middha)*, Doubt *(Vicikicchā)*, Ill Will *(Byāpāda)*, Restlessness or Worry *(Uddhacca-kukkucca)*, and Sensual Desire *(Kāmachanda)*. As the meditator approaches absorption, he or she perceives spontaneous *Nimitta* or signs of progress which are the tools of *Jhāna*. First, the meditator perceives *Parikamma Nimitta* or preliminary signs, signifying temporary or weak *(khaṇika) Samādhi*. With practice, these develop into an intermediate sign or *Uggaha-Nimitta*, when the sphere lasts for a short time. This signifies substantial or *Upacāra Samādhi*, which is already getting close to stable *Samādhi*. Finally, when the mind is permanently in the *Nimit*, the meditator comes to perceive the *Paṭibhaga Nimitta* or counterpart sign, signifying permanent *Samādhi*. At this stage, the meditator can control the *Nimitta*, moving it and changing its size.

At this point, the mind develops the Five *Jhāna* Virtues, each of which purifies the mind of the corresponding Hindrance. The *Jhāna* Virtues are Applied Thought or Attention *(Vitakka)* which purifies drowsiness or laziness; Sustained Thought or Contemplation *(Vicāra)* which purifies doubt; Joy or Rapture *(Pīti)* which purifies hatred or ill will; Peaceful Happiness *(Sukha)* which purifies Restlessness or Worry; and One-pointed Concentration *(Ekaggatā)* which purifies Sensual Desire or Enchantment. These five *Jhāna* Virtues all develop together quickly by the First *Jhāna* level. Applied Thought begins with the *Uggaha - Nimitta*, and the rest follow quickly with the *Paṭibhaga - Nimitta*.

When concentration and absorption develop further to the point where the mind no longer pays attention to either Applied or Sustained Thought, the meditator ascends into the Second *Jhāna,* where only Joy, Happiness and One-pointed Concentration remain active. Next, with further concentration and absorption, the mind no longer pays attention to Joy, and the meditator rises into the Third *Jhāna* with only Happiness and One-pointed Concentration. Thereafter, with further concentration and absorption, the mind no longer pays attention to Happiness, and there remains only One-pointed Concentration, which is joined by a new Virtue, Equanimity - neither happiness nor suffering. This is the Fourth *Jhāna.*

Question 5 : How does the meditator, then, continue to realize the Four Foundations of Mindfulness in *Samatha-Vipassanā* Meditation?

Answer 5 : Concentration of the mind at the 1st, 2nd, 3rd, and 4th levels of *Jhāna* causes development of a stable, concentrated mind purified from all hindrances. This is the necessary and sufficient preparation for direct comprehension of the Four Foundations of Mindfulness. The Pali wording for the Four Foundations of Mindfulness is *"anupassanā"* of the body-in-the-body, feelings-in-the-feelings, mind-in-the-mind, and "*Dhamma*-in-the-*Dhamma*." *"Anupassanā"* means step-by-step inner perception more than "contemplation." In step-by-step Meditation, this is carried out by actually seeing, knowing, and becoming successively more and more refined, purer and purer inner bodies, taking on their corresponding feelings, mental states and *Dhamma*. *Dhamma* is usually rendered as "mental objects" or "phenomena." As we have already noted, this refers to Lord Buddha's teachings: the Five Hindrances, Five Aggregates; Six Sense Organs and their sense-objects, the Seven Factors of Enlightenment, and the Four Noble Truths. As the meditator achieves the higher and higher levels of consciousness associated with the purer and more refined inner bodies, he or she attains deeper and deeper understanding of these teachings.

These more and more refined inner bodies are reborn or conceived spontaneously in natural accordance with Dependent Origination, as the meditator focuses the purified mind at the center of the center of the crude outer body. For example, in the First Jhāna, when one focuses attention at the center of the center of the body, the mind and *Dhamma*-in-the-*Dhamma* become purer and purer causing the Refined Human Body to emerge. Ignorance is still present but less active, and the high virtues of *Dāna* (sacrifice), *Sīla* (morality), and *Bhāvanā* (meditation) cause more refined and purer bodies to appear, together with their more blissful feelings *(Sukha Vedanā),* elevated mentality, and deeper comprehension of *Dhamma*. The meditator enters and becomes each body, in turn, using the higher capability of the new, elevated mind to reach the next body. The bodies are just the visible, attainable base supporting the higher virtue - the happier feelings, elevated mind, and deeper *Dhamma*.

The meditator is drawn naturally to leave the crude body behind and become the more blissful, refined body with purer mind and more profound *Dhamma*. Having become the Refined Human Body, meditation continues, concentrated at the center of the center of the Refined Human Body until the meditator perfects the virtues of this new, refined body and mind. Then, the center of the Refined Body expands itself and the next purer body - the Celestial Body - emerges with its even higher mental state of celestial virtues. The meditator becomes the Celestial Body, causing his or her mental phenomena to become even purer. In the same way, purer and purer refined bodies continue to pop up along with their more and more elevated feelings, purer and purer minds and more and more profound *Dhamma*, brought on by the higher and higher *Sīla*, *Samādhi* and *Paññā* of the successive bodies, which are all higher than the human level.

The meditator continues moving up step-by-step through all eight worldly bodies: Human, Refined Human, Celestial, Refined Celestial, Brahman, Refined Brahman, Formless Brahman, and the Refined Formless Brahman Body, which is the most refined of all the worldly bodies. The meditator becomes each body and uses its purer virtue and higher mentality to meditate up to the next level. When the meditator stops perfectly still at the center of the Refined Formless Brahman Body, the center expands itself and he or she meditates to *Dhammakāya.*

"*Dhamma*" means "Noble Level Virtue" and "*Kāya*" means body or base of the virtue. Lord Buddha said "*Dhammakāya itipi*" which means "*Dhammakāya* is me." The *Dhammakāya* Bodies support the supra-mundane virtues of the Noble Disciples, which form the path from the worldly level to *Nibbāna.* The body is what we can see, know and become. Each *Dhammakāya* is a radiant, crystal clear Buddha statue, sitting in meditation position inside a crystal sphere. Sitting down cross-legged, the statue is roughly the same height and width across the lap. There are a total of ten basic *Dhammakāya,* in pairs of crude and refined bodies, corresponding to path and fruit.

The First pair are the crude and refined *Gotrabhū Dhammakāya* which are roughly 9 meters in diameter. These are called "Noble State Wisdom." They are not yet at the Noble Disciple level. So long as the meditator cannot cut at least the first three of the Ten Fetters, he will still just stay in the *Gotrabhū* mentality, not yet to the Noble level.

Beyond *Gotrabhū,* one meditates to the level of the Nine Noble Virtues cited by Lord Buddha as 4 paths, plus 4 fruits, and plus 1 *Nibbāna.* The *Dhammakāya* are: *Sotābana* or Stream Enterer, Refined *Sotābana, Sakadāgāmi* or Once Returner, Refined *Sakadāgāmi, Anāgāmī* or Non-Returner, Refined *Anāgāmī, Arahant* or *Dhammakāya* Saint, and Refined *Arahant,* which is 40 meters in height and width. Finally, following this path, one can meditate to experience *Nibbāna* temporarily.

Question 6 : How does this *Samadha* Meditation practice prepare the meditator for *Vipassanā* Insight Meditation?

Answer 6 : At the Noble Disciple level, *Samadha* and *Vipassanā* Meditation already begin to merge. The meditator develops super normal tools for effective and efficient *Vipassanā* Meditation. These powers or *Abhiññā* such as the Angel Eye and Angel Ear, enable one to perceive the most refined beings and phenomena of the universe, which are transparent to the human eye and beyond the range of the human ear. One also develops the mental microscope and the mental telescope which enable seeing the whole universe and beyond to *Nibbāna.* These are the tools which facilitate *Samādha-Vipassanā* Meditation and enable one to follow Lord Buddha's development of the Three *Vijjā* which he attained on enlightenment night.

In conclusion, this time, we have explained *Samadha Meditation* in detail. Next time we will try a little practice. You will see that the practice is easier than the explanation.

Now I would like to wish all our listeners a very happy new year. May Lord Buddha bless you all to enjoy a fruitful, pleasurable, and profitable year with peace and joy throughout.

Interviewer : Thank you very much, Dr. Phra Rajyanvisith.

Chapter 3
Samadha or Concentration Meditation Practice

08 February 2008

Question 1: This is our eighth Sunday Dhamma Talk, now into our second year. We are currently discussing the three Higher Trainings which summarize the Noble Eightfold Path: First, *Adhisīla-sikkhā* or higher training in morality; Second, *Adhicitta-sikkhā* or Higher Mental Training, focusing on concentration meditation; and third, *Adhipaññā-sikkhā* or Higher Training in Wisdom, which focuses on *Vipassanā* or Insight Meditation. Last month, we discussed the theoretical aspects of the second Higher Training, *Adhicitta-sikkhā* or Higher Mental Training in *Samadha* or Concentration Meditation. This month we will devote our broadcast primarily to *Samadha* Meditation Practice.

Dr. Phra Rajyanvisith, welcome Venerable Sir. Could you please begin by summarizing the theoretical aspects of *Samadha* Meditation that we discussed last time. First, what benefits should one expect from *Samādhi* and *Samadha* Meditation?

Answer 1: *Samādhi,* or Concentration, is very useful in daily life, even for those who don't meditate formally. There are five concrete benefits.

First, concentration maintains and improves mental health, developing inner peace and tranquility which foster serenity, contentment and happiness.

Second, it engenders cool, calm composure, fostering self-possessed, rational behavior, unbiased judgement, and smooth, unruffled social interaction.

Third, concentration focuses thought, dispelling confusion and leading to more perceptive analysis and deeper insight.

Fourth, it maintains and improves physical health, providing rest and relaxation, averting sickness, and developing strength and vigor.

Finally, the fifth and ultimate benefit of concentration is cleansing out the Five Hindrances, which constrict our mental processes, in order to purify the mind to higher levels of consciousness. The Five Hindrances are: drowsiness or laziness, doubt or uncertainty, ill will or enmity, distraction or restlessness, and sensual desire or enchantment.

Samadha Meditation overcomes these hindrances and develops the mental tools for effective, objective observation of nature in *Vipassanā* or Insight Meditation to develop Right Wisdom. Vipassanā Meditation, then, permits the meditator to penetrate the Four Noble Truths to see clearly and compare objectively the compound, impermanent, unsatisfactory, suffering and hollow emptiness of this world with the non-compound, eternal, peacefully happy, and ultimately meaningful essence of *Nibbāna* or *Nirvana.*

Question 2 : Thank you, Venerable Sir. Now, please summarize what *Samādhi* is - what should we contemplate and what should we do.

Answer 2 : *Samādhi* or *Adhicittasikkhā* is higher mental training through Concentration Meditation, combining developing inner peace and concentration together. Lord Buddha listed nine effective subjects for *Samādhi* or Concentration Meditation: Four Foundations of Mindfulness - the body, feelings, mind and mental objects; Three inherent sufferings - old age, sickness, and death; One ultimate separation - the final parting from loved ones and ourselves; and One inevitable end result - the inescapable karmic consequences of our actions.

That is, the unavoidable natural law of cause and effect that determines our next rebirth. There is no way out. Only conscientious, consistently good behavior can save us.

Samadha Meditation covers three of the eight factors of the Noble Eightfold Path: (1) Right Effort, *Sammāvāyāma*; (2) Right Mindfulness, *Sammāsati;* and (3) Right Concentration, *Sammāsamādhi.*

The first factor, Right Effort, is defined as four exertions:

First, to prevent the arising of new bad habits of action, speech or thought, such as killing, stealing, sexual misconduct, addictions, lying and divisive speech, and evil intentions based on greed, lust, hatred, and deluded thinking.

The second effort is to abandon such bad habits as have already arisen.

The third is to develop new good habits, such as generosity and benevolence.

Finally, the fourth effort is to maintain good habits which have already arisen.

The second factor, Right Mindfulness, is defined as the Four Foundations of Mindfulness: successive inner perception *(anupassanā)* and contemplation of body, feelings, mental states, and *Dhamma* or true nature of reality. The meditator continues contemplating the body-in-the-body both internally and externally along with the arising and vanishing of phenomena in the body. He remains detached, being aware that there is body, without any clinging. Similarly, the meditator perceives and contemplates the feelings-in-the-feelings as pleasant, painful or neutral, without any clinging. Then, the meditator perceives and contemplates the mind-in-the-mind as lustful, hateful, deluded, distracted, developed, unsurpassed, concentrated, liberated, or the opposites of these states, again, without any clinging. Finally, the meditator perceives and contemplates the *Dhamma* in the *Dhamma*, or, specifically, the Five Hindrances; the Five Aggregates; the Six Sense Organs and their sense-objects; the Seven Factors of Enlightenment; and the Four Noble Truths.

Finally, mental training also covers Right Concentration or *Sammāsamādhi.* Samādhi is defined as developing the Four *Rūpa Jhānas* or States of Absorption, going deeper and deeper inside to purify the mind. The Venerable Commentator Phra Buddhaghosa has listed forty effective meditation devices, which fall into seven categories. They are: ten subjects for recollection *(Anusati)*, ten meditation objects *(Kasiṇa)*, ten ghastly sights *(Asubha)*, four divine qualities *(Brahmavihāra)*, four formless absorptions *(Arūpa Jhāna)*, one contemplation of food as garbage *(Āhāre paṭikūlasaññā)*, and analysis of the four elements *(Catudhātuvavaṭṭhāna)*. The Jhānas purify the mind from the Five Hindrances, which obscure clear-sightedness and transform the normal human senses into powerful instruments of observation, enabling the necessary and sufficient, reliable and valid collection of the relevant data required for direct, lucid comprehension of the true nature of reality.

Question 3 : Now, please tell us about the Four *Jhāna* or States of Absorption.

Answer 3 : The normal human mind is blurred by Five Hindrances. The Five Hindrances are Sleepiness or Laziness *(Thīna-middha)*, Doubt *(Vicikicchā)*, Ill will *(Byāpāda)*, Restlessness or Worry *(Uddhaccakukkucca)*, and Sensual Desire *(Kāmachanda)*. As the meditator approaches absorption, he or she perceives spontaneous *Nimitta* or signs of progress which are the tools of *Jhāna.* First, the meditator perceives *Parikamma Nimitta* or preliminary signs, signifying temporary or weak (*khaṇika*) *Samādhi.* With practice, these develop into an intermediate sign or *Uggaha-Nimitta*, when the sphere lasts for a short time. This signifies substantial or *Upacāra Samādhi,* which is already getting close to stable *Samādhi.* Finally, when the mind is permanently in the *Nimit,* the meditator comes to perceive the *Paṭibhaga*

Nimitta or counterpart sign, signifying permanent *Samādhi*. At this stage, the meditator can control the *Nimitta*, moving it and changing its size.

At this point, the mind develops the Five *Jhāna* Virtues, each of which purifies the mind of the corresponding Hindrance. The *Jhāna* Virtues are Applied Thought or Attention *(Vitakka)* which purifies drowsiness or laziness; Sustained Thought or Contemplation *(Vicāra)* which purifies doubt; Joy or Rapture *(Pīti)* which purifies hatred or ill will; Peaceful Happiness *(Sukha)* which purifies Restlessness or Worry; and One-pointed Concentration *(Ekaggatā)* which purifies Sensual Desire or Enchantment. These five *Jhāna* Virtues all develop together quickly by the First *Jhāna* level. Thereafter, the meditator ascends to the second, third and fourth *Jhāna* as the mind becomes more refined, purer and more stable.

Question 4: How does the meditator, then, continue to realize the Four Foundations of Mindfulness in *Samatha-Vipassanā* Meditation?

Answer 4: Concentration of the mind at the various *Jhāna* levels develops a stable, concentrated mind purified from hindrances. This is the necessary and sufficient preparation for direct comprehension of the Four Foundations of Mindfulness. The Pali wording for the Four Foundations of Mindfulness is *"anupassanā"* of the body-in-the-body, feelings-in-the-feelings, mind-in-the-mind, and *"Dhamma*-in-the-*Dhamma."* *"Anupassanā"* means successive inner perception more than "contemplation." In *Samadha-Vipassanā* Meditation, this is carried out by actually seeing, knowing, and becoming successively more and more refined, purer and purer inner bodies, taking on their corresponding feelings, mental states and *Dhamma*. As the meditator achieves higher and higher levels of consciousness, he or she attains deeper and deeper understanding of *Dhamma*. The meditator uses the higher capability of each new, elevated mind to reach the next body.

The bodies are just the visible, attainable base supporting the higher virtue, happier feelings, elevated mind, and deeper *Dhamma*. The meditator is drawn naturally to leave the crude body behind and become the more blissful, refined body with purer mind and more profound *Dhamma*. Thus, the meditator continues moving up step-by-step through all eight worldly bodies and ten *Dhammakāya* bodies, which encompass the crude and refined Noble Disciples - the Stream Enterer or *Sotāpanna*, Once Returner or *Sakadāgāmī*, Non-Returner or *Anāgāmī* and the *Dhammakāya* Saint or *Arahant*, which is 40 meters in height and width.

At the Noble Disciple level, the meditator develops super-normal tools such as angel vision, angel hearing, the mental telescope and the mental microscope which facilitate effective and efficient *Vipassanā* Meditation.

Question 5 : Now, can you please lead us in a brief introduction to *Samadha* Meditation?

Answer 5 : [10-11 minutes of meditation]

We sit upright in a regular meditation posture (see Figure 1 on page 34), cross-legged as seen in some Buddha images, with the right leg resting upon the left. The right hand rests on the left, palms turned upwards, with the right index finger just touching the left thumb. The body is straight and the mind is fully alert. Take a deep breath and relax the body until you feel comfortable. Close your eyelids lightly, do not press them.

Figure 1 : The Meditation Posture

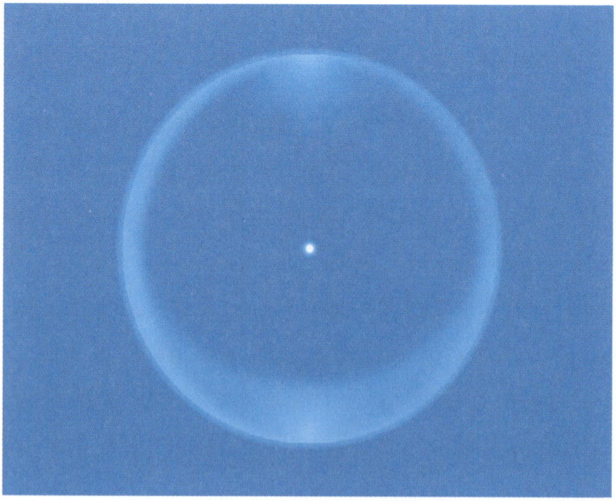

Figure 2 : The Object of Visualization

In basic *Samadha* practice, we use two aids: the repeated word or mantra (*Parikamma-bhāvanā*) and the object of visualization (*Parikamma-nimitta*). The repetitive word is *"Sammā Arahang"* which is *Buddhānusati* or remembrance of the Buddha's virtues, from the *Anusati* category of meditation devices. The object of visualization is a bright, clear luminous sphere called the *Āloka Kasiṇa* or light object, from the *Kasiṇa* meditation devices. Using these aids, we draw the mind inward to the center of the body. Such concentration allows the mind components of vision, memory, thought and awareness to come together into oneness.

Begin by mentally imagining a bright, clear, luminous sphere located just outside your nostril aperture - right at the opening of the nose - for ladies on the left side, and for gentlemen on the right side. This is the first base at which the mind pauses. Focus your full attention at the center of the sphere so that the four components of the mind - which are Sensation, Memory, Thought and Cognition - come together at one point together with the sphere. It is a natural phenomenon that whenever you see any object with your mind, these four components of the mind are functioning together, along with that object. When you see the sphere, these four mental components are functioning together with the sphere, and when you focus your mind at the center of the sphere, they all come

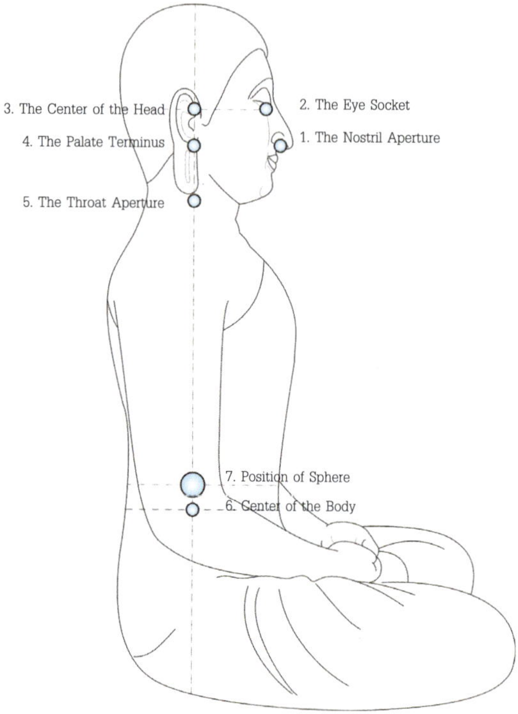

Figure 3 : The Path to the Center of the Body

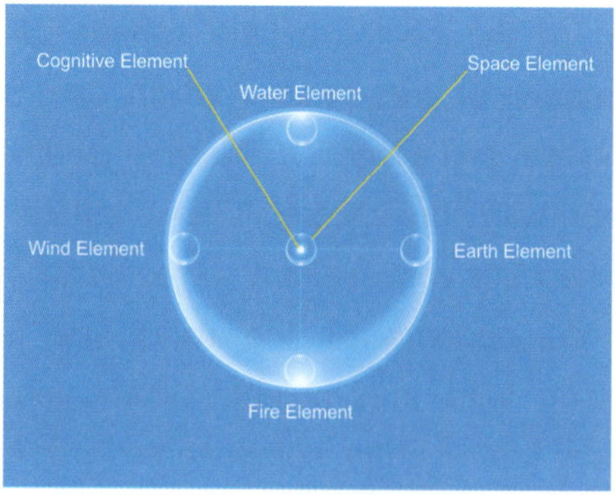

Figure 4 : The Sphere at the Center of the Body and the Elements together at that one point. This is the way we calm and concentrate our mind. The mind itself is invisible, but we can use visible objects to train it.

While your mind is concentrated at the center of the sphere, recite over and over to yourself the mantra or repeated words *"Sammā Arahang, Sammā Arahang, Sammā Arahang."* This is *Buddhānusati* or recollection of the Buddha's virtues. *"Sammā"* is the Pali word for "Right," meaning ultimately correct or True. It is the first word of each of the factors in the Noble Eightfold Path - Right speech, Right Action, Right Livelihood, etc. Here, we use it as an abbreviation for "*Sammāsam-buddho*" meaning Lord Buddha's Enlightened Wisdom. This recollection amounts to making the wish "May I gain wisdom." The second word of the mantra is *"Arahang"* meaning "purity." It constitutes remembrance of Lord Buddha's spotless freedom from defilements and amounts to the wish "May I gain purity."

Now, keeping your mind at the center of the sphere, mentally move the sphere slowly, smoothly, and gently inside the nose, upward through the nose, and over into the eye socket - for ladies on the left side and for gentlemen on the right side. Don't worry about the sphere fitting inside the nose - mental objects do not have to fit into physical objects. Rest the sphere in the eyesocket and recite *"Sammā Arahang"* to yourself three times. This is the second base for pausing the mind. *"Sammā Arahang, Sammā Arahang, Sammā Arahang."*

Next, still keeping your mind at the center of the sphere, bring the sphere backward to the center of the head, at eye level. This is the third base. Rest the sphere there and repeat "*Sammā Arahang*" three times. "*Sammā Arahang, Sammā Arahang, Sammā Arahang.*"

From here, we begin to move the sphere downwards. It helps to roll the eyeballs up slightly - just gently, not too much. Keeping our mind at the center of the sphere, we move the sphere straight to the pallet terminus - the back of the roof of the mouth. Rest the mind there. This is the fourth base for pausing the mind. Repeat "*Sammā Arahang*" three times. "*Sammā Arahang, Sammā Arahang, Sammā Arahang.*"

We continue our downward journey, bringing the sphere straight downward to the opening of the throat - the Throat Aperture. Keep your mind at the center of the sphere, and rest the sphere there. This is the fifth base for pausing the mind. Repeat "*Sammā Arahang*" three times. "*Sammā Arahang, Sammā Arahang, Sammā Arahang.*"

From here, we make the long move straight down to the center of the body at the navel level - behind the belly button. You can imagine a bright, thin, clear line from the belly button straight back to the backbone, and another line crosswise from left to right. These lines meet at the center of the body. You can also visualize a third line right down the center of the body, through the throat, crossing the first two. This is the path down which we move the sphere. Slowly, smoothly, gently - down, down, down, down. Keep your mind always at the center of the sphere, and bring the sphere to rest at this sixth base of the mind. Repeat "*Sammā Arahang*" three times. "*Sammā Arahang, Sammā Arahang, Sammā Arahang.*"

Finally, we make our last short move back upwards, the way we came. Keeping our mind at the center of the sphere, we move the sphere back up the central pathway to be just about two inches or five centimeters above the belly button. This is the seventh and final base of the mind. This is where we will always meditate in the future. We won't move the mind anywhere further. Position Seven is the center of the body. If you take a few deep breaths and observe the breath going down inside the body, you will see it passes the Position Number Seven and ends at the navel. Rest your mind inside the sphere at Position Number Seven, and Repeat "*Sammā Arahang*" three times. "*Sammā Arahang, Sammā Arahang, Sammā Arahang.*" We have arrived.

This is the mind's permanent resting place. Whenever a person or any other creature is born, dies, sleeps, or wakens, the *Dhamma* Sphere which governs the body arises from this position. The *Dhamma* Sphere is composed of the Sensation Sphere, the Memory Sphere, the Thought Sphere, and the Cognition Sphere. Keep the bright sphere resting at the center of the body. Mentally recite the words *Sammā Arahang* continuously to keep the sphere still and make it become brighter and clearer. Focus your mind at the bright center of the sphere, and at the bright center of each successive sphere that emerges. Pay no attention to any external sensation. Do not force the mind too strongly. Do not use the physical eyes to focus on the vision. Always focus on the center of each new sphere which emerges. Rest the mind there.

Eventually, a bright clear sphere will arise. This is the *Dhamma* Sphere. Do not be overjoyed. Keep your mind calm in equanimity. Hold the mind still, and stop repeating *Sammā Arahang*. Just concentrate at the center of the Dhamma sphere. This is your own nucleus which gives rise to this body and this mind. You should feel that your mind is in the very purest state it has ever achieved, with firm oneness. You should experience the greatest happiness that you have ever known - not happiness based on an external object, but happiness arising from within. This is due to being fully pure from the Five Hindrances.

If you continue to focus the mind at the center of the center of each successive sphere, the center expands itself naturally. Initially, you see sphere after sphere. Ultimately, you will come to see some refined body. Usually, this is the refined human body, which looks like yourself, but is much nicer and is transparent. At this point, you may begin to observe some supernormal abilities such as super-normal vision and hearing. The mind is now alert, razor-sharp, and fully prepared for *Vipassanā* Meditation.

[Brief pause.]

And now, let us share all of the merit that we have made in this meditation and previously - together with all of our loving kindness - with all beings everywhere throughout the universe. We share with our parents, our grandparents, our family, our teachers and our friends. We share with our King and our Queen and the whole royal family - especially with the King's elder sister, who has recently passed on. And, we also share with any enemies - anyone with whom we may have disagreement. Let us always remember that we are all brothers and sisters together, here in this world of suffering - through birth, old age, sickness and death. We share with all celestial beings - the angels, the devas, and the brahmans. We share with all the animals and with the beings suffering in Hell, including the ghosts and the demons. May Lord Buddha bless us all to lead a peaceful, happy life, free from suffering, free from problems and free from enmity, and may this meditation help to bring us closer to transcendence and Nirvana. [pause.] And, now, we come slowly out of meditation and open the eyes.

Interviewer : Thank you very much, Dr. Phra Rajyanvisith. You have taught us a lot and opened new doors.

Phra Rajyahvisith : May Lord Buddha be with you all.

Chapter 4

Paññā or Vipassanā of the Three Characteristics

02 March 2008

Question 1: This is our ninth Sunday Dhamma Talk. For several broadcasts, we have been addressing the three Higher Trainings - *Sīla* or Moral behavior, *Samādhi* or Concentration, and *Paññā* or gaining Wisdom through *Vipassanā* Insight Meditation. These Three Trainings summarize the Eightfold Path. Last month, we completed dealing with *Sīla* and *Samādhi* by focusing on *Samadha* Meditation Practice.

This Sunday we begin discussion of the third training on *Paññā* or Wisdom. Welcome, Venerable Dr. Phra Rajyanvisith. Could you please begin by summarizing our previous session for our listeners, to show how *Samadha* practice leads on to *Vipassanā* and the development of Wisdom?

Answer 1: Good morning and welcome, ladies and gentlemen. *Samadha* Meditation covers three of the eight factors of the Noble Eightfold Path: Right Effort, *Sammāvāyāma*; Right Mindfulness, *Sammāsati*; and Right Concentration, *Sammāsamādhi*. The main benefit of Samadha meditation is developing the five *Jhāna* Virtues to cleanse the mind of the Five Hindrances: Applied Thought *(Vitakka)* purifies drowsiness; Sustained Thought *(Vicāra)* purifies doubt; Joy *(Pīti)* purifies ill will; Happiness *(Sukha)* purifies Restless Mind; and One-pointed Concentration *(Ekaggatā)* purifies Sensual Desire.

The *Jhānas* develop a stable, concentrated mind purified from the Five Hindrances and effective and efficient tools for direct comprehension (*Anupassanā*) of the Four Foundations of Mindfulness: body-in-the-body, feelings-in-the-feelings, mind-in-the-mind, and *Dhamma*-in-the-*Dhamma*, learning thru direct experience to compare the characteristics of compound phenomena (such as the Five Aggregates) with the non-compound phenomenon of Nirvana. In *Samadha-Vipassanā* Meditation, this is carried out by actually seeing, knowing, and becoming successively more and more refined, purer and purer inner bodies, taking on their corresponding feelings, mental states and perception of *Dhamma*.

Question 2: What is *Vipassanā* Meditation? What are its objectives and what is the general approach?

Answer 2: The Higher Training in Wisdom *(Adhipaññā-sikkhā)* aims at developing the insight to see clearly and compare objectively the true nature of conditioned phenomena, such as the Five Aggregates, with the ultimate reality of the unconditioned phenomenon of Nirvana or *Nirodha Dhātu*. This is *Vipassanā* Meditation. It can be best achieved when the mind has already been trained to become pure and firmly concentrated through *Samadha* Meditation.

There are two levels of Insight or *Vipassanā* Meditation. The first level is called *Anupassanā*. It is clear comprehension of the three universal characteristics of all compound phenomena - that they are impermanent, suffering, and non-self (that is, empty and meaningless). These characteristics must be understood in comparison with the opposite characteristics of non-compound phenomena which are eternal, supreme happiness, and ultimate reality. This is the first level of *Vipassanā* Meditation. This is what we will study today.

The second level of Insight or *Vipassanā* Meditation is detailed contemplation of the Four Noble Truths in three transcendent mental states *(Ñāṇa)*: *Sacca Ñāṇa*, *Kicca Ñāṇa*, and *Kata Ñāṇa*. In *Sacca*

Ñāṇa, the meditator becomes able to see clearly and really know objectively suffering, the arising of suffering, the cessation of suffering, and the path leading to the cessation of suffering. In *Kicca Ñāṇa,* he comes to know clearly what he is supposed to do with respect to each of the Four Noble Truths. First, suffering *(Dukkha)* should be gotten rid of; Second, the cause of suffering *(Samudaya)* should be abandoned or relinquished; Third, the cessation of suffering (*Nirodha*) should be clearly realized or penetrated; Fourth, the path *(Magga)* should be entered upon, practiced, and developed. Finally, in *Kata Ñāṇa*, the meditator sees clearly the progress that he has already achieved. This is *Gotrabhū Ñāṇa*. From there, if the meditator can cut at least the first three fetters, which are false self concept, doubt and reliance on ineffective rituals, he can immediately experience the non-compound nature of Nirvana. We will deal with this aspect of *Vipassanā* in the next broadcast.

Question 3 : Now, please explain *Anupassanā*, clear comprehension of the origin and true nature of compound phenomena.

Answer 3 : Compound phenomena are made up of visible, physical components and invisible factors which influence birth and development. Everything in this world is compound. There are two main types of compound phenomena - living and non-living. We shall focus on living phenomena, which encompass all the characteristics and factors. Specifically, let's focus on ourselves, understood as the Five Aggregates of Body, Sensation, Memory, Thought and Recognition.

Like all compound phenomena, we are born, exist for a time, and then die and disintegrate. While in existence, we change, constantly, first growing and then degenerating. We exhibit the three universal characteristics of impermanence *(Aniccang)*, suffering *(Dukkhang)*, and non-self *(Anattā)*. These three qualities are, in fact, only three different perspectives on the same trait - impermanence. With attachment, impermanence is experienced as suffering, because we are inevitably separated from what we love and united with what we detest. Similarly, impermanence implies "Non-self" in the sense of being void of real, permanent essence.

Our rebirth is fundamentally conditioned by ignorance. We want to be reborn because we love it here. It is nourished by the passions: greed or lust, hatred or anger, and delusion or misconception. These passions stimulate wholesome or unwholesome behaviors which produce either beneficial or harmful karmic consequences through actions, words and motives. Good actions, such as making merit, may result in fortunate births, but as long as ignorance remains, rebirth will continue. Three main factors govern our rebirth. They are Karma, consciousness, and craving.

Good or bad resultant Karma *(Vipāka Kamma)*, based on past actions, causes us to be reborn into the happy or suffering worlds. The happy worlds are the Human, Celestial, Brahman and Formless Brahman Worlds. They all provide substantial opportunities for further progress. The suffering worlds are the worlds of Animals, Demons, Hungry Ghosts, and Hell Beings. In these worlds, one is essentially cut off from opportunities for advancement, only paying off debts.

Our consciousness or cognition factor *(Viññāṇa)* determines what we can see and comprehend. It acts like a seed that flourishes throughout our growth and development. Our craving, whether wholesome or unwholesome, is the life force that propels germination and growth. This presentation has been a brief summary of Conditioned Genesis *(Paṭiccasamupāda)*, which we will study in detail later on.

When a human being dies, it is the coarse human body that we see cease to function. The four mental aggregates and the refined human body, which are all transparent, along with the karmic accumulation from the last lifetime, constitute the microscopic nucleus for a new psycho-physical organism. They all depart together from the crude body as it passes away.

If its virtues, such as generosity *(Dāna)* and morality *(Sīla)*, fall into the human range, the nucleus prepares for a human rebirth. It enters the body of the potential father, following the seven-step path that we learn in meditation, and comes to rest at the center of the body. Here, the nucleus can wait up to seven days. Its merits influence the father to have sexual desire for the mother. When the mental aggregates of the father, mother, and baby come together, a human force similar to gravity pulls the baby from the father into the mother as the sperm joins the egg. This is why our mental spheres are at the center of the body.

This is the original microscopic origin of the embryo. The four material essences (Water, Earth, Fire and Wind) develop into the crude meat and bones of the baby's body, while the four mental elements remain perfectly still and pure, never opening the gate for passion. This is the initial development of the baby's body and mind.

After birth, the remaining karma will function at its appropriate time. While growing up, the human mind always wanders outside and attaches to worldly objects, which may be good or bad, causing either wholesome or unwholesome effects. The mind may be stirred up or calm, stupid or wise, depraved or virtuous, leading to suffering or happiness. The physical elements (Earth, Fire, Water, and Wind) will be active in the young, causing growth, but less powerful in the elderly, causing the body to degenerate. The hair falls out, the teeth become loose, the skin becomes wrinkled, etc. Thus, we see that the body is impermanent, suffering, and unsatisfactory. In the end, it disintegrates and becomes non-self. In conclusion, we see that the body is void of any permanent, happy, self essence.

Question 4 : Thank you very much, sir. Now, can you please explain how to conduct insight meditation to compare compound and non-compound phenomena?

Answer 4 : We begin with Four Foundations of Mindfulness meditation to experience and contemplate the bodies-in-the-body, feelings-in-the-feel-ings, mind-in-the-mind, and *Dhamma*-in-the-*Dhamma*. The meditator devel-ops *Jhāna* to purify the mind from Hindrances. Once the mind is pure and firmly concentrated, the meditator begins by contemplating the coarse physical human body, observing the five "root" (*mūla*) meditation objects. These are the hair on the head, body hair, finger and toe nails, teeth, and skin.

Let's take the hair on the head as an example. The meditator takes a single hair from the top of the head and examines it as though under a microscope at the center of the body. He sees the hair as it really is - impure and subject to change, in accordance with the factors influencing it, such as food and environment. With age, it naturally becomes less healthy and may turn grey or white. He notes that hair is impermanent. It may fall out, and will ultimately disintegrate, becoming no longer hair. It is, thus, impermanent *(Aniccang)* and unsatisfactory *(Dukkhang).* And, it is void of permanent reality or ultimate significance. It is, thus, "Non-self" or *Anattā*, not the eternal self of anyone.

The same thing can be said for the hair on the body. Similarly, the teeth are impure - bathed in bacteria, smelly, subject to cavities, and apt to break and fall out. So, too, our nails need constant care - cleaning and clipping. The skin is always covered with sweat, needing to be bathed and have its stink covered over with perfumes. All of these body parts are impure, subject to change, unsatisfactory and potential sources of suffering. They are impermanent, without ultimate reality or meaning. This is the true nature of the whole body. From our birth as a baby, we develop until the prime of life, and then degenerate, growing old, suffering, becoming sick, and dying. After examining the physical body, the meditator continues with the four mental aggregates: Sensation, Memory, Thought and Cognition. Ultimately, this leads to clear comprehension that this whole psycho-physical organism is Non-self *(Anattā).*

Anupassanā, thus, leads to comprehending the ultimate reality of the Five Aggregates as suffering and elucidates the cause of suffering as Craving and Attachment. When the meditator can let go, he can experience extinction of suffering, which is *Gotarabhū Ñāṇa*. If he meditates further, he may experience Nirvana, which is non-compound and has the characteristics of eternal permanence, supreme peaceful happiness, and ultimate reality. He will, then, be able to compare the characteristics of compound and non-compound phenomena and realize the superiority and accessibility of the latter. This is Right Wisdom *(Paññā)* which can eventually lead to enlightenment in the Four Noble Truths.

Question 5 : Now, can you please lead us in a brief Vipassanā Meditation using the *Anupassanā* approach of examining the Three Characteristics.

Answer 5 : [6-7 minutes of meditation] We sit upright in a regular meditation posture, cross-legged as seen in some Buddha images, with the right leg resting upon the left. The right hand rests on the left, palms turned upwards, with the right index finger just touching the left thumb. The body is straight and the mind is fully alert. Take a deep breath and relax the body until you feel comfortable. Close your eyelids lightly, do not press them.

We use two aids: First, a mantra, repeated over and over again. Our mantra is *"Sammā Arahang."* Second, an object of visualization, a bright, clear luminous sphere called the *Āloka Kasiṇa* or light object. Using these aids, we draw the mind inward to the center of the body, and the mind components of Sensation, Memory, Thought, and Cognition come together into oneness.

Imagine a bright, clear, luminous sphere located at the sixth base of the mind, the center of your body, directly behind the navel or belly button. Focus your full attention at the center of the sphere, so that the four components of the mind - Sensation, memory, thought and Cognition - come together at one point inside the sphere. This is the way we calm and concentrate our mind. The mind itself is invisible, but we can use visible objects to train it.

You can imagine a bright, thin, clear line from the navel straight back to the backbone, and another line crosswise from left to right. These lines meet at the center of the body. You can also visualize a third line right down the center of the body, through the throat, crossing the first two. This defines the center of the body.

While your mind is concentrated at the center of the sphere, recite the mantra over and over to yourself - "*Sammā Arahang, Sammā Arahang, Sammā Arahang.*" This is *Buddhānusati* or recollection of the Buddha's virtues. *"Sammā"* is the Pali word for "Right," meaning ultimately correct or True. It is an abbreviation for *"Sammāsambuddho"* meaning Lord Buddha's Enlightened Wisdom. This amounts to making the wish "May I gain wisdom." The second word of the mantra is *"Arahang"* meaning "purity." This is remembering Lord Buddha's spotless freedom from defilements and amounts to the wish "May I gain purity."

From the navel level, we bring the sphere upwards just two inches or five centimeters, keeping our mind at the center of the sphere. This is the final, seventh base of the mind, referred to as the "position of the sphere" at the center of the body. Rest your mind inside the sphere at Position Seven, and Repeat "*Sammā Arahang, Sammā Arahang, Sammā Arahang, Sammā Arahang*" continually and mindfully.

This is the mind's permanent resting place. Whenever a person or any other creature is born, dies, sleeps or wakens, the *Dhamma* Sphere arises at the center of the body or *Rūpa Khanda*. Inside the *Dhamma* Sphere are five little spheres of the original elements. At the front, the Water Element; to the right, the Earth Element; at the back, the Fire Element; and on the left, the Wind Element. At the center is the Space Element, and inside the Space Element are the four mind aggregates, located concentrically inside each other. Namely, the spheres of Sensation, Memory, Thought and Cognition. Thus, the four mind aggregates are located at the center of the body aggregate.

Keep the bright sphere resting at the center of the body. Mentally recite the words *Sammā Arahang* continuously to keep the sphere still and make it become brighter and clearer. Focus your mind at the bright center of the sphere, and at the bright center of each successive sphere that emerges. Pay no attention to any external sensation. Do not force the mind too strongly. Do not use the physical eyes to focus on the vision. Always focus on the center of each new sphere which emerges. Rest the mind there.

Eventually, a bright clear sphere will arise. This is the *Dhamma* Sphere. Do not be overjoyed. Keep your mind calm in equanimity. Hold the mind still, and stop repeating *Sammā Arahang*. Just concentrate at the center of the *Dhamma* sphere. This is your own nucleus which gives rise to this body and this mind. You should feel that your mind is in the very purest state it has ever achieved, with firm oneness. You should experience the greatest happiness that you have ever known - not happiness based on an external object, but happiness arising from within. This is due to being fully pure from the Five Hindrances.

Now, take one hair from the top of your head and visualize it as under a microscope at the center of your sphere at the center of the body. Take a good look. See it as it really is. Look how dirty it is. Look at the natural processes of degeneration constantly at work to make it look and smell bad. We think we are stuck with this body. In meditation, however, we can enjoy our celestial, angel body, radiant with cheerful brightness, gentle loving kindness, and warm compassion. Ultimately, we can meditate to experience the non-compound nature of Nibbāna or Nirvana - eternal, peaceful happiness and essential, meaningful reality. That is where we belong. That is our refuge. [Brief pause.]

And now, let us share all of the merit that we have made in this meditation and previously - together with all of our loving kindness - with all beings everywhere throughout the universe. We share with our parents, our grandparents, our family, our teachers and our friends. We share with our King and our Queen and the whole royal family - especially with the King's elder sister, who has recently passed on. May Lord Buddha bless us all to lead a peaceful, happy life, free from suffering, free from problems and free from enmity. And may this meditation help to bring us closer to transcendence and Nirvana. [pause.] And, now, we come slowly out of meditation and open the eyes.

Interviewer : Thank you very much, Dr. Phra Rajyanvisith. We all deeply appreciate your very kind and generous instruction.

Phra Rajyanvisith : May Lord Buddha bless you all.

Interviewer : We would like to invite interested listeners to join us for meditation at Wat Luang Phor Sodh any Sunday. Our bus leaves from just outside the entrance of Wat Saket, the Golden Mountain Temple, at 07:00 every Sunday morning, and returns to Wat Saket around 16:00 hours. Dr. Phra Rajyanvisith leads morning chanting and meditation in Thai, beginning at 09:30, and I conduct a meditation session, separately, for English speakers. You are all very welcomed. Please see our website at ***www.dhammacenter.org*** for more details.

Chapter 5

The Four Foundations of Mindfulness
No. 1 Body

06 April 2008

Question 1: This is our tenth Sunday *Dhamma* Talk. We are into the third Higher Training, *Paññā* or developing Wisdom through *Vipassanā* Insight Meditation. We are now going to begin to discuss the details of Lord Buddha's major message on meditation, The Greater Discourse on the Four Foundations of Mindfulness. Today, we shall consider the first of the Four Foundations: Mindfulness of the Body. Venerable Dr. Phra Rajyanvisith, I have the honor to wish you a very good morning. Could you please begin by summarizing briefly our previous session for those who missed it.

Answer 1: Good morning, ladies and gentlemen. The Higher Training in Wisdom *(Adhipaññā-Sikkhā)* aims at developing the insight to see clearly and grasp firmly the true nature of this world's ephemeral, illusory conditioned phenomena. These include the Five Aggregates of body, Sensation, Memory, Thought and Cognition which make up our own psycho-physical organism or *Nāmarūpa*. Meditators penetrate to full comprehension through objective comparison of conditioned phenomena with the ultimate, eternal, unchanging reality of Nirvana which is everlasting or immortal. This is *Vipassanā* Meditation. It can be best achieved when the mind has already been trained to become pure and firmly concentrated through *Samadha*.

Compound phenomena include both visible, physical components and invisible factors, such as Karma, which influence birth and development. Everything in this world is compound, including our own Five Aggregates. We are born, exist for a moment, and then die and disintegrate. While in existence, we change constantly, first growing and then degenerating. We exhibit the three universal characteristics of impermanence *(Aniccaṃ)*, suffering *(Dukkhaṃ)*, and non-self *(Anattā)*.

Our rebirth is fundamentally conditioned by ignorance, nourished by the passions - greed, hatred, and delusion - which stimulate behaviors producing either beneficial or harmful karmic consequences. As long as ignorance remains, rebirth will continue. Rebirth into happy or suffering worlds is governed by three main factors. First, "Niche" Karma or *kammaṃ khettaṃ* is favorable or unfavorable destiny based on past actions, which determines the happy or suffering nature of one's specific slot in the new world. Second, "Seed"

Consciousness or *Viññāṇam Bijaṃ* establishes the genetic base or root stock determining what we can see and comprehend. Finally, "Germination" Craving or *Taṇhā Sineho* imparts the life force propelling growth. These three factors condition "becoming." First, they create the world and specific niche into which the new being will be born, and then they produce rebirth. old age, sickness and death - in brief "suffering" - follow automatically.

When a human being dies, it is the coarse human body that we see cease to function. The four mental aggregates and the inner refined human body, together with the karmic accumulations form the nucleus for a new psycho-physical organism. They all depart together from the crude body as it passes away. If the virtues of this nucleus fall into the human range, it prepares for human rebirth, entering the body of the potential father and waiting at the center of the body for up to seven days for the potential parents to have sexual intercourse. When the mental aggregates of father, mother, and baby come together, a human force similar to gravity pulls the baby from the father into the mother as the sperm joins the egg. This is why our mental spheres are at the center of the body.

Question 2 : Thank you, sir. Now, can you please explain Mindfulness of the Body Meditation, the first of the Four Foundations of Mindfulness.

Answer 2 : We conduct Four Foundations of Mindfulness Meditation to experience and contemplate successive Bodiy-in-the-body, Feelings-in-the-feelings, Mind-in-the-mind, and *Dhamma*-in-the-*Dhamma.* The meditator, first, practices *Samadha* Meditation to develop *Jhāna* and purify the mind from the Five Hindrances: laziness, doubt, ill will, restlessness, and sensual desire. When the mind is pure and firmly concentrated, the seeker reflects on the coarse human body by observing the five "root" meditation objects, which are the hair on the head, body hair, nails, teeth, and skin.

From these five, the meditator can expand to contemplating all 32 parts of the body designated for study. These are: head-hairs, body-hairs, nails, teeth, skin, flesh, sinews, bones, marrow, kidneys, heart, liver, pleura, spleen, lungs, intestines, intestinal tract, stomach, faeces, bile, phlegm, pus, blood, sweat, fat, tears, grease, saliva, nasal mucus, synovium (oil lubricating the joints), urine and the brain in the skull. These 32 parts of the body all have the universal worldly characteristics of being impermanent, subject to suffering, and "non-self" or voidness of real, permanent essence. We can observe these characteristics internally in our own body and also externally in the bodies of others. This is the first level of Mindfulness of the Body.

As meditation progresses to higher and higher levels, we can also examine refined bodies-in-the-body, transcendent *Dhammakāya*, and eventually, the ultimate ageless, immortal, supreme peace and happiness of Nirvana. As we compare the unsatisfactory, frustrating, mundane characteristics of worldly phenomena with the splendid radiance, peace and happiness of transcendent *Dhammakāya* and Nirvana, wisdom blossoms. We penetrate ultimate, absolute realization that everything in this world, including our own psycho-physical organism, is just an ephemeral, enchanting, deluding, frustrating and ultimately tormenting fantasy. We become bored with the chores of taking care of the body - continually feeding, washing, grooming and nursing it. As one meditator commented, the body comes to seem like a heavy backpack that we are always carrying. It feels so good when we put it down.

Such insight releases us from attachment and frees us from bodily cravings as well as the passions and unwholesome actions which cause suffering. Wisdom and purity develop hand-in-hand. As wisdom develops, the mind becomes purer and purer, more and more peaceful, and able to see more and more clearly, inspiring Right Speech, Right Action, and Right Livelihood which result in peaceful, happy living. At the same time, Right Wisdom enables the meditator to fulfill the Ten Perfections, cutting the Fetters binding us to this sensual world and transcending to higher and higher *Dhammakāya* levels.

The first *Dhammakāya* body, *Gotrabhū,* is the gatekeeper with one foot in transcendence and one foot in the sensual world. *Gotrabhū* has not yet reached Noble Disciple level and can still fall back to be swallowed up in the engulfing flood of sensual enchantment again. With continuing practice, the meditator advances to Stream Enterer and then to higher and higher Noble Disciple *Dhammakāya* with purer and purer virtues. These *Dhammakāya* eventually appear permanently, giving broad insight and Right Wisdom, leading the crude human body to behave properly with Right Speech, Right Action, and Right Livelihood. This, also, develops the other factors of the Noble Eightfold Path: Right Effort, Right Mindfulness, Right Concentration, Right Thought, and Right Intention. These terminate accumulation of bad Karma and add momentum to the upward spiral, enhancing Right Wisdom, cutting more Fetters, and reaching higher and higher Noble Disciple levels. We experience less and less craving and attachment; enjoy more and more freedom from suffering; and ultimately cut all Ten Fetters to reach Arahant sainthood.

Question 3 : Thank you, sir. Now, can you please detail the specific methods for conducting Mindfulness of the Body Meditation.

Answer 3 : Lord Buddha specifies six methods for contemplating the body:

[1] The first method is Contemplation of Breathing *(Ānāpānasati).* A bhikkhu sits cross-legged in a solitary place, keeping his body erect, and focuses on breathing. Only with keen mindfulness he breathes in and breathes out. Breathing in a long breath or a short breath and breathing out a long breath or a short breath, he knows what he is doing. He trains himself to be aware of the whole breath body and to calm the breathing process. He dwells, perceiving the body, over and over again, as just body (not mine, self, or "I," but just as a phenomenon). He perceives the body as just body both in himself and in others. He perceives the arising and dissolution of the body, along with their causes. He is firmly mindful that only body exists. There is no soul, self or "I." Progressively, he gains insight *(Vipassanā)* and becomes detached from craving and wrong views. Thus, he dwells without clinging to anything in this world.

[2] The second method is Mindfulness of Body Postures *(Iriyāpatho).* A bhikkhu is always mindful of Body Postures, whether walking, standing, sitting, or lying

down. Whatever way his body is moving or placed, he dwells perceiving the body, again and again, as just body, and dwells without clinging to anything in this world.

[3] The third method is Full Awareness of Bodily Actions *(Sampajaññaṃ).* A bhikkhu is always fully aware of what he is doing, whether moving forward or backward, looking straight ahead or elsewhere, bending or stretching, or while eating, drinking, chewing, tasting, urinating or defecating. He is fully aware while walking, standing, sitting, falling asleep, waking, speaking, or remaining silent. He is firmly mindful that this is only body, and dwells without clinging to anything in this world.

[4] The fourth method is Contemplating the Body as Impure *(Paṭikūla-manasikāro)* A bhikkhu examines the body piece-by-piece, from the soles of the feet to the tip of the hair on the head, as just a bag of skin full of pollutants. He repeats the 32 parts of the body over and over, firmly mindful that this is only body, he dwells without clinging to anything in this world.

[5] The fifth method is Contemplation of the Body as Just Elements. *(Dhātu manasika).* Again, a *bhikkhu* examines and analyzes the body as only a collection of primary elements, thinking that this body consists only of the earth element, the water element,

the fire element, and the air element. He is firmly mindful that this is only body, he dwells without clinging to anything in this world.

[6] The sixth method is The Nine Contemplations of Decaying Corpses *(Navasivathikā).*

(1) First, a bhikkhu contemplates a body one to three days dead - swollen, blue and festering, thinking that this body, too, will become like that;

(2) Second, a body being devored by crows, vultures, other animals, and worms;

(3) Third, a skeleton held together by tendons, with some flesh and blood still adhering to it;

(4) Fourth, a skeleton held together by tendons and blood-smeared, but fleshless;

(5) Fifth, a skeleton held together by tendons, but without either flesh or blood;

(6) Sixth, a body that is just loose bones scattered in all directions;

(7) Seventh, a body that is just conch-colored bleached bones;

(8) Eighth, a body that is bones over a year old, lying in a heap;

(9) Finally, ninth, a bhikkhu contemplates a body that is just rotted bones, crumbling to dust. He thinks that this body, too, will become like that. It cannot escape it. Thus, he dwells, perceiving the body as just body (not mine, self, or "I", but just a phenomenon). He perceives the body as just body in both himself and in others. He perceives the arising and dissolution of the body and the causes for each. He is firmly mindful that only body exists, no soul, self or "I". Mindfulness leads to insight and he becomes detached from craving and wrong views. He dwells without clinging to anything in this world. These are the ways in which a bhikkhu dwells perceiving, again and again, the body as just body.

Question 4 : Now, sir, can you please lead us in a few minutes of Mindfulness of the Body *Vipassanā* Meditation.

Answer 4 : We sit upright in a regular meditation posture, cross-legged as seen in some Buddha images, with the right leg resting upon the left. The right hand rests on the left, palms turned upwards, with the right index finger just touching the left thumb. The body is straight and the mind is fully alert. Take a deep breath and relax the body until you feel comfortable. Close your eyelids lightly, do not press them.

We use two aids: First, a mantra, repeated over and over again. Our mantra is *"Sammā Arahang."* Second, an object of visualization, a bright, clear luminous sphere called the *Āloka Kasiṇa* or light object. Using these aids, we draw the mind inward to the center of the body, and the mind components of Sensation, Memory, Thought and Cognition come together into oneness.

Imagine a bright, clear, luminous sphere located at the sixth base of the mind, the center of your body, directly behind the navel or belly button. Focus your full attention at the center of the sphere, so that the four components of the mind - Sensation, Memory, Thought and Cognition - come together at one point inside the sphere. This is the way we calm and concentrate our mind. The mind itself is invisible, but we can use visible objects to train it.

While your mind is concentrated at the center of the sphere, recite the mantra over and over to yourself - "*Sammā Arahang, Sammā Arahang, Sammā Arahang.*" This is *Buddhanusati* or recollection of the Buddha's virtues. *"Sammā"* is the Pali word for "Right," meaning ultimately correct or True. It is an abbreviation for "*Sammāsambuddho*" meaning Lord Buddha's Enlightened Wisdom. This amounts to making the wish "May I gain wisdom." The second word of the mantra is "*Arahang*" meaning "purity." This is remembering Lord Buddha's spotless freedom from defilements and amounts to the wish "May I gain purity."

From the navel level, we bring the sphere upwards just two inches or five centimeters, keeping our mind at the center of the sphere. This is the final, seventh base of the mind, referred to as the "Position of the Sphere" at the center of the body. Rest your mind inside the sphere at Position Number Seven, and Repeat "*Sammā Arahang, Sammā Arahang, Sammā Arahang*" continually and mindfully.

This is the mind's permanent resting place. Whenever a person or any other creature is born, dies, sleeps or wakens, the *Dhamma* Sphere arises at the center of the body. Inside the *Dhamma* Sphere are five little spheres of the original elements. At the front, the Water Element; to the right, the Earth Element; at the back, the Fire Element; and on the left, the Wind Element. At the center is the Space Element, and inside the Space Element are the four mind aggregates, located concentrically inside each other. Namely, the spheres of Sensation, Memory, Thought and Cognition. Thus, the four mind aggregates are located at the center of the body aggregate.

Keep the bright sphere resting at the center of the body. Mentally recite the words *Sammā Arahang* continuously to keep the sphere still and make it become brighter and clearer. Focus your mind at the bright center of the sphere, and at the bright center of each successive sphere that emerges. Pay no attention to any external sensation. Do not force the mind too strongly. Do not use the physical eyes to focus on the vision. Always focus on the center of each new sphere which emerges. Rest the mind there.

Eventually, a bright clear sphere will arise. This is the *Dhamma* Sphere. Do not be overjoyed. Keep your mind calm in equanimity. Hold the mind still, and stop repeating *Sammā Arahang*. Just concentrate at the center of the *Dhamma* sphere. This is your own nucleus which gives rise to this body and this mind. You should feel that your mind is in the very purest state it has ever achieved, with firm oneness. You should experience the greatest happiness that you have ever known - not happiness based on an external object, but happiness arising from within. This is due to being fully pure from the Five Hindrances.

Now, take one hair from the top of your head and visualize it as under a microscope at the center of your sphere at the center of the body. Take a good look. See it as it really is. Look how dirty it is.

Look at the natural processes of degeneration constantly at work to make it look and smell bad. We think we are stuck with this body. In meditation, however, we can enjoy our Celestial, Angel Body, radiant with cheerful brightness, gentle loving-kindness, and warm compassion. Ultimately, we can meditate to experience the non-compound nature of Nibbana or Nirvana - eternal, peaceful happiness and essential, meaningful reality. That is where we belong. That is our refuge.

[Brief pause.]

And now, let us share all of the merit that we have made in this meditation and previously - together with all of our loving-kindness - with all beings everywhere throughout the universe. We share with our parents, our grandparents, our family, our teachers and our friends. We share with our King and our Queen and the whole Chakri Dynasty - especially with the King's elder sister, who has recently passed on. May Lord Buddha bless us all to lead a peaceful, happy life, free from suffering, free from problems and free from enmity. And may this meditation help to bring us closer to transcendence and Nirvana. [pause.] And, now, we come slowly out of meditation and open the eyes.

Interviewer : Thank you very much, Dr. Phra Rajyanvisith. We all deeply appreciate your very kind and generous instruction.

Phra Rajyanvisith : May Lord Buddha bless you all.

Interviewer : We would like to invite all interested listeners to join us for meditation at Wat Luang Phor Sodh any Sunday. Our bus leaves from just outside the entrance of Wat Saket, the Golden Mountain Temple, at 07:00 every Sunday morning. Dr. Phra Rajyanvisith leads morning chanting and meditation in Thai, beginning at 09:30, and I conduct a meditation session, separately, for English speakers. You are all very welcomed. Please see our website at ***www.dhammacenter.org*** for details.

Chapter 6

The Four Foundations of Mindfulness: No. 2 & 3 Feelings and Mind

04 May 2008

Question 1: This is our eleventh Sunday *Dhamma* Talk. We are continuing with the third Higher Training, *Paññā* or Wisdom, developed through *Vipassanā* Insight Meditation. Lord Buddha's fundamental presentation on meditation is the Greater Discourse on the Four Foundations of Mindfulness. The Four Foundations of Mindfulness are Mindfulness of Body, Mindfulness of Feelings, Mindfulness of Mind, and Mindfulness of *Dhamma* or Mental Objects.

We began studying the Four Foundations of Mindfulness last time, by considering the first foundation, Mindfulness of Body. Today we will discuss the second and third of the Four Foundations, Mindfulness of Feelings and Mindfulness of Mind. Good morning, Venerable Dr. Phra Rajyanvisith. We bid you welcome and look forward to more of your erudite wisdom. As usual, please begin by summarizing our previous broadcast which focused on Mindfulness of Body.

Answer 1: Good morning, ladies and gentlemen. All of our presentations to date have shown repeatedly that there is more to life than meets the eye. Life is both broader and more refined than the visible spectrum. Invisible truths of nature such as the Law of Karma and Rebirth underlie what we see everyday. At death, it is only the coarse outer body which disintegrates. The refined inner bodies and minds continue, seeking rebirth. Rebirth is conditioned by ignorance and nourished by the passions - greed, hatred, and delusion. It is governed by three main factors. First, "Niche" Karma or *Kammaṃ Khettaṃ* based on past actions; second, "Seed" Consciousness or *Viññāṇṃ Bijam*, which determines what we can see and comprehend; and, third, "Germination" Craving or *Taṇhā Sineho* which is the life force propelling growth.

Last time we began reflecting on the Four Foundations of Mindfulness by examining "Mindfulness of Body." The approach to "Mindfulness of Body" mental training provides the template for the other three Foundations: experiencing successively more and more refined bodies-in-the-body, feelings-in-the-feelings, mind-in-the-mind, and *dhamma*-in-the-*dhamma*. The goal is developing the insight to penetrate the "Three Universal Characteristics" of this world's ephemeral, illusory, and hollow phenomena, which simply arise when conditions are right, exist briefly changing continually while in existence, and then dissipate. Most vital is lucid comprehension that this fleeting insubstantiality is our own intrinsic nature. It is the essential quality of the Five Aggregates - Body, Sensation, Memory, Thought, and Cognition - which we generally consider our "selves." Meditators achieve such transcendence through objective comparison of the impermanence *(Aniccang)*, suffering *(Dukkhang)*, and non-self *(Anattā)* of worldly phenomena - in particular, our Five Aggregates - with the eternal, soothing, and ultimate reality of Nirvana. This is *Vipassanā* Meditation. It is best achieved through preparation with *Samadha* (i.e., *Jhāna)* and *Anupassanā* (i.e., Four Foundations of Mindfulness) Meditation.

The template for Four Foundations of Mindfulness or *Anupassanā* Meditation consists of four steps. In Step 1, meditation begins with concentration into *Jhāna* for the Five *Jhāna* Factors to overcome the Five Hindrances which distort and limit our everyday consciousness. First, Applied Thought *(Vitakka)* overcomes sleepiness and laziness *(Thīna-middha);* Second, Sustained Thought *(Vicāra)* overcomes doubt *(Vicikicchā);* Third, joy *(Pīti)* overcomes ill will *(Byāpāda);* Fourth, contented happiness *(Sukha)* overcomes restlessness *(Uddhacca-kukkucca);* and, Fifth, concentration *(Ekaggatā)* overcomes sensual enchantment *(Kāmachanda).*

In Step 2, the meditator focuses on the body, feelings, mind or mind objects of this current "Crude Human Body." For body, he begins with the Five Root Meditation Objects (head hair, body hair, teeth, nails, and skin) and expands to "The 32 Parts of the Body," contemplating that all are impure and impermanent, subject to suffering, and non-self. The meditator examines these characteristics both internally, in himself, and externally in the bodies of others. Lord Buddha details six specific methods for Mindfulness of Body Meditation: (1) Contemplation of Breathing *(Ānāpānasati)*, (2) Mindfulness of Body Postures *(Iriyāpatho)*, (3) Full Awareness of Bodily Actions *(Sampajaññaṃ)*, (4) Contemplating the Body as Impure *(Paṭikūla manasikāro)*, (5) Contemplation of the Body as Just Elements. *(Dhātu manasikāro)*, and (6) The Nine Contemplations of Decaying Corpses *(Navasivathikā)*.

In Step 3, one progresses to higher levels with the mind stopped still at the center of the crude outer body, becoming and experiencing the body, feelings, mind or mind objects of successively higher and more refined inner bodies-in-the-body. The meditator first progresses through the worldly bodies, which reflect *Jhāna*. There are four worldly levels - Human (corresponding to First *Jhāna*), Celestial (corresponding to Second *Jhāna*), Brahman (corresponding to Third *Jhāna*), and Formless

Brahman (corresponding to Fourth *Jhāna*). But, at each level there are two bodies - Crude, reflecting Path, and Refined, reflecting Fruit.

Beyond the worldly level, the meditator transcends to the *Dhammakāya* plane, first becoming *Dhammakāya Gotrabhū* or Noble State Wisdom. *Dhammakāya Gotrabhū* is the gatekeeper at the entrance to transcendence. From this level, the meditator continues to ascend through the Noble Disciple stages, becoming Stream Enterer *(Sotāpanna)*, Once Returner *(Sakadāgāmī)*, Non-Returner *(Anāgāmī)* and, ultimately, *Dhammakāya* Saint *(Arahant)*, each with purer and purer virtues. With practice, each *Dhammakāya* comes to appear permanently, giving broad insight, leading the Crude Human Body to behave properly, ending accumulation of bad karma and adding momentum to the upward spiral. This accelerating whirl enhances Right Wisdom, cuts Fetters, reduces craving and attachment, and generates increasing freedom from suffering.

In Step 4, one, ultimately, becomes *Dhammakāya* Arahant, capable of experiencing Nirvana or *Nibbāna* directly during meditation. This permits direct, personal experience and comparison of the eternal, blissful, ultimate reality of Nirvana with the ephemeral, illusory, hollow delusions of this world. At this point, Lord Buddha often says that the Noble Disciple becomes bored with this world, gives up all attachment, and attains enlightenment.

Question 2 : Thank you very much, sir. Now, can you explain how one practices Mindfulness of Feelings?

Answer 2 : Today we are focusing on Mindfulness of Feelings and Mind. It should be noted that one does not have to contemplate all four types of mindfulness. Whenever one can penetrate through to see clearly the cause of the arising of the Five Aggregates, that is sufficient for attaining the path and fruit of Nirvana and penetrating the Four Noble Truths. When a meditator begins concentration of mind and reaches the *Dhamma* sphere or nucleus, this is already *Jhāna,* the absorption developing pure mind. One experiences feelings changing from the crude outer body to refined status. Suffering, *Dukkha*, becomes Happiness, *Sukha*. For example, when one sits a long time without developing concentration, one feels the hurting of the legs. This is suffering. When the mind is perfectly concentrated, the virtues of the Five *Jhāna* Factors wipe out the Five Hindrances and the hurt in the legs disappears. This hurting in the legs can be termed as one of the Five Hindrances - either doubt, feeling ill at ease, or ill will, etc. These are eliminated in the First *Jhāna.*

Meditating is doing good. The merit earned causes happier feelings. Thus, one experiences impermanence *(Aniccang)* in an upward direction. When there is no concentration, the mind wanders outside, building more attachments. The closest thing is one's own body, so the mind immediately attaches to it. But, when the mind is concentrated and free from attachment to the body, this leads to happier feelings. As one concentrates more and more on the nucleus sphere, one delves deeper and deeper into the Spheres of *Sīla, Samādhi, Paññā, Vimutti* and *Vimutti-Ñāṇadassana.* Then, comes the Refined Human Body. Over and over again, the meditator is led to leave behind that which feels crude or uncomfortable and become the more and more refined and blissful bodies. The merit from the new purity of morality *Sīla* and concentration *Samādhi* helps the meditator feel happier and freed from the former suffering of the crude body as well as from hindrances and attachment. The mind becomes pure. This peacefully pure and concentrated quality of mind *(Samādhi)* is one of the keystone "Foundations of Mindfulness", along with the Right Wisdom of knowing what causes suffering *(Paññā)* and good behavior or *Sīla*.

Mindfulness of feelings is being aware of the freedom from suffering that one experiences as *Sīla*, *Samādhi*, and *Paññā* all develop together. It can be that good behavior, *Sīla*, produces purer mind, which leads to Right Wisdom. In another way, *Paññā* develops *Sīla* and *Sīla* develops *Samādhi*. In brief, all three assist one another and develop simultaneously, along with Right Wisdom in the Four Noble Truths *(Paññā).* There can be both ups and downs. This is readily noted in daily life experience. One must be continually mindful during both meditation and daily life. Doing good develops the mind and makes one happier and purer. These are the benefits from good behavior. One must always avoid evil, do good, and purify the mind.

Now, to complete my answer, here is how Lord Buddha taught "Mindfulness of Feelings". A bhikkhu* feeling a pleasant, unpleasant or neutral feeling knows that he is experiencing a pleasant, unpleasant, or neutral feeling. If the feeling is based on sense pleasures, he knows that it is based on sense pleasures. Thus he dwells perceiving again and again feelings as just feelings (not mine, not I, not self, but just as phenomena). He perceives this in himself and in others. He dwells perceiving the cause and appearing of feelings; or the cause and dissolution of feelings. He is firmly mindful that only feelings exists (not soul, self or I). Knowing that mindfulness of feelings is just for progressively developing more insight and mindfulness, he remains detached from craving and wrong view and dwells without clinging to anything in the world. In this way the bhikkhu dwells perceiving again and again feelings as just feelings.

---

* bhikkhu means a Buddhist monk who observes the 227 precepts of discipline.

Question 3 : Thank you again, Sir. And, how does one practice Mindfulness of Mind?

Answer 3 : Lord Buddha taught Meditation for Mindfulness of Mind as follows. When a mind with greed, anger, delusion, laziness or distraction arises, the bhikkhu knows, that this is a mind with greed, anger, delusion, laziness or distraction. Similarly, when a mind free of greed, anger, delusion, laziness or distraction arises, he knows that this is a mind free of greed, anger, delusion, laziness or distraction. He perceives this both in himself and in others.

When a developed or undeveloped, superior or inferior, concentrated or un-concentrated mind arises, the bhikkhu knows that this is a developed or undeveloped, superior or inferior, concentrated or un-concentrated mind. Similarly, when a mind temporarily free from defilements or not free from defilements arises, he knows that this is a mind temporarily free from defilements or not free from defilements. Thus he dwells perceiving again and again mind as just mind (not mine, not I, not self but just a phenomenon.) He perceives this both in himself and in others. He dwells perceiving the cause and appearing of mind or the cause and dissolution of mind. He is firmly mindful that only mind exists (not soul, self or I). Mindfulness of mind is just for progressively developing more insight and mindfulness, he remains detached from craving and wrong view, and dwells without clinging to anything in the world. In this way, the bhikkhu dwells perceiving again and again mind as just mind.

Question 4 : And now, sir, can you please lead us in a few minutes of Mindfulness of Feelings and Mind *Anupassanā* Meditation.

Answer 4 : We sit upright in a regular meditation posture, cross-legged as seen in some Buddha images, with the right leg resting upon the left. The right hand rests on the left, palms turned upwards, with the right index finger just touching the left thumb. The body is straight and the mind is fully alert. Take a deep breath and relax the body until you feel comfortable. Close your eyelids lightly, do not press them. Before we start, take a moment to feel and note any discomfort you may be feeling in the legs, back, shoulders, neck, or elsewhere. Remember how that discomfort feels. Also, please evaluate your current level of peace and happiness of mind. This will be our baseline for later comparison.

We use two aids: First, a mantra, repeated over and over again. Our mantra is *"Sammā Ara-hang."* Second, an object of visualization, a bright, clear luminous sphere called the *Āloka Kasiṇa* or light object. Using these aids, we draw the mind inward to the center of the body, and the mind components of Sensation, Memory, Thought and Cognition come together into oneness. Imagine a bright, clear, luminous sphere located at Position Seven, in the center of the body, two inches or five centimeters above the navel. This is Position Seven, the position of the sphere at the center of the body. Rest your mind inside the sphere and Repeat "*Sammā Arahang, Sammā Arahang*" continually and mindfully. This is *Buddhānusati* or recollection of the Buddha's virtues. "*Sammā*" is the Pali word for "Right," meaning ultimately correct or True. It is an abbreviation for "*Sammāsambuddho*" meaning Lord Buddha's Enlightened Wisdom. This is making the wish "May I gain wisdom." The second word of the mantra is "*Arahang*" meaning "purity." This is remembering Lord Buddha's spotless freedom from defilements and is the wish "May I gain purity."

Mentally recite *Sammā Arahang* continuously to keep the sphere still and make it brighter and clearer. Pay no attention to any external sensation. Do not force the mind too strongly. Do not use the physical eyes, only the mind's eye that dreams. Look for the pinpoint of bright light at the center of the center. Focus your mind there. Stop Still. Feel the stillness. The mind stops still. The body stops still. Stop still at the center of the center. And, when the mind stops, perfectly still, at the center of the center, the center expands itself and becomes a new sphere. Place your mind gently inside the new sphere. Look for the pin point of bright light at the center of the center. Place your mind there. Stop still. Stop still and wait. Wait for the whole mind to stop, perfectly still. The center expands itself. Sphere after sphere, center after center, over and over, deeper and deeper, brighter and brighter, closer and closer to the center of the center.

Eventually, a bright clear sphere will arise. This is the *Dhamma* Sphere. Do not be overjoyed. Keep your mind calm in equanimity. Hold the mind still, and stop repeating *Sammā Arahang*. Just concentrate at the center of the *Dhamma* sphere. This is your own nucleus which gives rise to this body and this mind. Inside the *Dhamma* Sphere are five little spheres of the original elements. At the front, the Water Element; to the right, the Earth Element; at the back, the Fire Element; and on the left, the Wind Element. At the center is the Space Element, and inside the Space Element are the four mind aggregates, located concentrically inside each other - the spheres of Sensation, Memory, Thought and Cognition. Thus, the four mind aggregates are located at the center of the body aggregate. You should feel your mind at the very purest state it has ever achieved, with firm oneness. You should experience the greatest happiness you have ever known - not happiness based on an external object, but happiness arising from within, due to being fully pure from the Five Hindrances. Take a brief moment of silence to enjoy the peace and happiness of being concentrated at the center of the *Dhamma* Sphere. [Pause.]

Now, think back to the discomfort you felt and noted back in the beginning. Is it still there, or has it gone away? If you have succeeded in reaching and entering the *Dhamma* Sphere, you will find that it has disappeared. Likewise, evaluate the peaceful happiness of your current state of mind. Is it the same, better, or worse than when you started? Most of you will feel more peaceful and happier, even from just a few minutes of meditation. This is a benefit of meditation that all can appreciate. It is not far from this level, that we have already reached, to the Celestial Body where heavenly feelings of joy are almost overpowering.
[Brief pause.]

And now, let us share all of the merit that we have made in this meditation and previously - together with all of our loving-kindness - with all beings everywhere throughout the universe. We share with our parents, our grandparents, our family, our teachers and our friends. We share with our King and our Queen and the whole royal family - especially with the King's elder sister, who has recently passed on. May Lord Buddha bless us all to lead a peaceful, happy life, free from suffering, free from problems and free from enmity. And may this meditation help to bring us closer to transcendence and Nirvana. [Pause.] And, now, we come slowly out of meditation and open the eyes.

Interviewer : Thank you very much, Dr. Phra Rajyanvisith. We all very deeply appreciate your kind and generous instruction.

Phra Rajyanvisith : May Lord Buddha bless you all. We would like to invite all of you to join us for meditation at Wat Luang Phor Sodh any Sunday. Our bus leaves from just outside the entrance of Wat Saket, the Golden Mountain Temple, at seven o'clock every Sunday morning. I lead morning chanting and meditation for all, beginning at nine thirty, and Phra Bart conducts an afternoon meditation session in English from twelve to two P.M. You are all very sincerely invited. Please come join us. See our website at ***www.dhammacenter.org*** for details.

Chapter 7

The Four Foundations of Mindfulness : No. 4 : Dhamma

01 June 2008

Question 1 : This is our twelfth Sunday Dhamma Talk, completing one year of broadcasts. Today we shall finish consideration of Lord Buddha's main sermon on meditation, the "Greater Discourse on the Four Foundations of Mindfulness." The Four Foundations are Mindfulness of Body, Feelings, Mind, and *Dhamma* or Mental Objects. Today, we shall study the fourth of these, *Dhamma*.

This will also conclude our series on the three Higher Trainings or *Adhisikkhā* which are *Sīla* or moral behavior, *Samādhi* or concentration meditation, and *Paññā* or transcendental Wisdom achieved through through *Vipassanā* insight meditation.

Good morning, Dr. Phra Rajyanvisith. Welcome Venerable Sir. We are all delighted to have you back with us again. As usual, sir, I would like to ask you to begin by summarizing our previous broadcast on Mindfulness of Feelings and Mind.

Answer 1: Good morning, ladies and gentlemen. Last time we considered Mindfulness of Feelings and Mind. We used "Mindfulness of Body" as a template, experiencing more and more refined bodies-in-the-body, feelings-in-the-feelings, mind-in-the-mind, and *Dhamma*-in-the-*Dhamma*, in order to penetrate the "Three Universal Characteristics" of all worldly phenomena. As meditators, we can compare the impermanence *(Aniccang)*, suffering *(Dukkhang)*, and non-self *(Anattā)* of mundane phenomena with the eternal, supreme happiness, ultimate reality of Nirvana. We must comprehend that fleeting insubstantiality is our own intrinsic nature. This is *Vipas-sanā* Meditation, best achieved through preparation with *Samadha* meditation to *Jhāna* and *Anupassanā* or Four Foundations of Mindfulness Meditation.

Four Foundations of Mindfulness Meditation begins with concentration to *Jhāna* level to overcome the Five Hindrances. Second, the meditator focuses on the body, feelings, mind or Mind Objects of his current "Crude Human Body." Third, one progresses to more refined inner "bodies-in-the-body," experiencing the body, feelings, mind and mind objects of each. Transcending to the *Dhammakāya* plane, the meditator ultimately becomes *Dhammakāya Arahant,* capable of experiencing *Nibbāna* directly during meditation. This permits direct, personal comparison of the eternal, blissful, ultimate reality of Nirvana with the ephemeral, illusory, hollow delusions of this world. At this point, Lord Buddha often says that the Noble Disciple becomes bored with this world, gives up all attachment, and attains enlightenment.

Question 2 : Thank you very much, sir. Now, can you please explain how one practices Mindfulness of *Dhamma*.

Answer 2 : Today we will consider Mindfulness of the *Dhamma*-in-the-*Dhamma* in order to penetrate through to seeing clearly the cause of the arising of the Five Aggregates, that is, to understand the reason for the rebirth of the psycho -physical organism *(Nāmarūpa)*. This insight is sufficient for attaining the path and fruit of Nirvāṇa and penetrating the Four Noble Truths.

The word *Dhamma* has many meanings - Nature, Truth, Lord Buddha's teachings, and, more broadly, "mental objects." In the Four Foundations of Mindfulness context, it has always been translated as "mental objects." This is not wrong, but it is a bit vague. When we look, closely at what Lord Buddha would have us contemplate, we find a specific list of five items: [1] First, the five Hindrances or *Nīvaraṇa*, [2] Second, the five Aggregates or *Khanda*, [3] Third, the six Sense Organs and six Sense Objects or *Āyatana*, [4] Fourth, the seven Factors of Enlightenment or

Bojjhaṅga, and [5] Fifth, the Four Noble Truths *(Ariyasacca).* It is clear that *Dhamma*, here, means contemplation of "Teachings" rather than all mental phenomena. This focuses our task and makes it do-able. In English, this is reflected by capitalizing the word *Dhamma*.

Penetrating to lucid comprehension of the *Dhamma* - the True Nature of Reality as perceived by Lord Buddha during enlightenment - has been our real ultimate goal all along. Climbing the ladder of refined bodies was really just a technique for raising our level of consciousness, step-by-step, to develop the ability to comprehend and internalize these lessons. Developing *Dhammakāya* is the fulfillment of achieving this capability. The meditator raises consciousness through consecutive Noble Disciple stages to *Dhammakāya Arahant* level, competent to experience *Nibbāna* directly, during meditation to compare compound and non-compound nature with true, relevant, valid, and reliable data. Thus, we are finally down to our ultimate task of penetrating Lord Buddha's *Dhamma,* which is also our own internal *Dhamma*, culminating in the Four Noble Truths. These are the final steps to enlightenment.

Let us summarize, briefly, the essence of each of the five meditations detailed in the *Mahā Satipaṭṭhāna Sutta*. Regarding the Five Hindrances, one must be aware of the Five Hindrances and prevent and remove them through *Samadha* meditation to attain *Jhāna*. First, Applied Thought *(Vitakka)* overcomes sleepiness and laziness *(Thīna-middha);* Second, Sustained Thought *(Vicāra)* overcomes doubt *(Vicikicchā);* Third, joy *(Pīti)* overcomes ill will *(Byāpāda);* Fourth, contented happiness (*Sukha*) overcomes restlessness *(Uddhacca-kukkucca);* and, Fifth, concentration *(Ekaggatā)* overcomes sensual enchantment *(Kāmachanda).*

Regarding the Five Aggregates or *Khanda* which make up our psycho-physical organism *(Nāma-rūpa),* they are Body *(Rūpa),* Feelings or Sensations *(Vedanā),* Memory *(Saññā),* Thought *(Saṅkhāra)* and Cognition *(Viññāṇa).* The meditator must be aware of attachment to these *Khanda* and carefully analyze them to see them as they really are - ephemeral, frustrating, and illusory.

Similarly, with respect to the six Sense Bases (the eye, ear, nose, tongue, body, and mind) and their Sense Objects (sights, sounds, smells, tastes, tangible objects and mental objects), meditators must examine them in detail to understand their true nature as Impermanent, Subject to Change, and Non-self. This helps to develop Right Wisdom with respect to the Three Universal Characteristics *(Tilakkhaṇa)* of all Compound Things.

Next, the meditator contemplates the seven *bhojjaṅga* as just the seven factors of enlightenment to be developed, not mine, not I, not self, but just as phenomena. When the enlightenment factor of mindfulness *(Sati-sambojjhaṅga)* is present, he knows it is present. When it is not present, he knows it is not present. He also knows how it arises and how complete development of it comes to be. He is similarly aware regarding the enlightenment factors of investigation of phenomena *(Dhamma-vicaya-bojjhaṅga),* effort *(Viriya-sambojjhaṅga),* rapture *(Piti-sambojjhaṅga),* tranquility *(Passaddhi-sambojjhaṅga),* concentration *(Samādhi-sambojjhaṅga),* and the enlightenment factor of equanimity *(Upekkhā-sambojjhaṅga).* Thus, he dwells perceiving again and again *dhammas* as just *dhammas* (not mine, not I, not self, but just as phenomena) in himself. Being detached from craving and wrong views, he dwells without clinging to anything in the world.

Finally, the meditator contemplates the *Four Noble Truths* in similar fashion, to see them as they really are and to develop the right wisdom to understand what should be done. First, regarding the Truth of Suffering *(Dukkha),* he contemplates birth, aging, death, sorrow, lamentation, physical pain, mental pain, anguish, being associated with persons and things that one dislikes, being separated from persons and things that one likes, wishing for what one cannot get, aging, sickness, and death. And, at last, he contemplates the Five Aggregates of Clinging as *Dukkha*.

Second, regarding the Cause of Dukkha, *Samudaya*, he ponders over craving, rebirth, delight, clinging, sense pleasures, craving for a better existence and craving for non-existence. He contemplates that craving and clinging arise where there is pleasurable feelings. This means at the six sense bases. When sense-contact yields pleasurable feeling, craving arises and leads to volitional intention.

Third, regarding *Nirodha, Nirodha* is the cessation of the causes of *Dukkha* and *Dukkha* itself, the complete extinction of craving, abandoning and discarding it. One achieves liberation and detachment from it. Craving is abandoned wherever delight and pleasure are found. That is, craving is abandoned in the six sense bases. When craving is discarded, volition is also abandoned, applied thought is deserted, and sustained thought is also cast off. This is the cessation of *Dukkha*.

Fourth, the meditator contemplates the Noble Eightfold Path *(Magga):* Right View, *(Sammādiṭṭhi)*, Right Thought *(Sammāsaṅkappa)*, Right Speech *(Sammā-vācā)*, Right Action *(Sammākammanta)*, Right Livelihood *(Sammāājīva)*, Right Effort *(Sammāvāyāma)*, Right Mindfulness *(Sammāsati)*, and Right Concentration *(Sammā-*

samādhi). With Right Concentration, and detached from sensual desire and unwholesome states, he attains and dwells in the first *Jhāna*; then the second *Jhāna;* the third *Jhāna;* and the fourth *Jhāna*. This is a state of pure mindfulness born of equanimity. It is Right Concentration. And, that is the Noble Truth of the Path leading to the cessation of *Dukkha*.

The meditator contemplates these Four Noble Truths in three transcendent mental states *(Ñāṇa):* (1) In *Sacca Ñāṇa* he penetrates to lucid direct knowledge of suffering, the cause of suffering, *Nibbāna*, and the Path to *Nibbāna*. (2) In *Kicca Ñāṇa* he achieves the Right Wisdom to know what to do regarding each of the Four Noble Truths. He must divest himself of *Dukkha*, give up craving, realize *Nibbāna,* and keep to the Path. (3) Finally, in *Kata Ñāṇa*, the meditator recognizes that he has already achieved these tasks. This is *Gotrabhū Ñāṇa*, the first of the transcendental *Dhammakāya* states. From there, when the meditator can cut at least the first three of the ten Fetters, which are false self concept, doubt and reliance on ineffective rituals, he can immediately experience the non-compound nature of *Nibbāna.*

Lord Buddha said, "Whoever practices these four *Satipaṭṭhāna* for seven years can expect either immediate Arahantship or the state of Non-returner *(Anāgāmī).*

... Forget seven years, whoever practices these four *Satipaṭṭhāna* for seven months, can expect either Arahantship or Non-Returner status. ... Forget seven months, whoever practices these four *Satipaṭṭhāna* ...for only seven days can expect one of two results: Arahantship in this very existence or the state of Non-Returner *(Anāgāmī)*. Thus, the four *Satipaṭṭhāna* are the one-way highway to the purification of the minds of beings, for overcoming sorrow and lamentation, for the cessation of physical and mental pain, for the attainment of the Noble Path, and for the realization of *Nibbāna*.

Question 3 : Thank you again, sir. Now, can you please lead us in a brief *Anupassanā* Meditation.

Answer 3 : Today we will meditate farther than before. We will continue on to the bodies. Please be very alert and concentrated.

We sit upright in a regular meditation posture, cross-legged as seen in some Buddha images, with the right leg resting upon the left. The right hand rests on the left, palms turned upwards, with the right index finger just touching the left thumb. The body is straight and the mind is fully alert. Take a deep breath and relax the body until you feel comfortable. Close your eyelids lightly, do not press them.

We use two aids: First, a mantra, repeated over and over again. Our mantra is *"Sammā Arahang."* Second, an object of visualization, a bright, clear luminous sphere called the *Āloka Kasiṇa* or light object. Using these aids, we draw the mind inward to the center of the body, and the mind components of Sensation, Memory, Thought and Cognition come together into oneness. Imagine a bright, clear, luminous sphere located at Position Seven, in the center of the body, two inches or five centimeters above the navel. This is Position seven, the position of the sphere at the center of the body. Rest your mind inside the sphere and Repeat *"Sammā Arahang, Sammā Arahang"* continually and mindfully. Look for the pinpoint of bright light at the center of the center. Focus your mind there. Stop Still. Feel the stillness.

When the mind stops, perfectly still, at the center of the center, the center expands itself and becomes a new sphere. Place your mind gently inside the new sphere. Look for the pin point of bright light at the centre of the center. Place your mind there. Stop still. Eventually, a bright clear sphere will arise. This is the Dhamma Sphere. Do not be overjoyed. Keep your mind calm in equanimity. Hold the mind still, and stop repeating *Sammā Arahang*. Just concentrate at the center of the Dhamma sphere. This is your own nucleus which gives rise to this body and this mind.

You should feel your mind at the very purest state it has ever achieved, with firm oneness. You should experience the greatest happiness you have ever known - not happiness based on an external object, but happiness arising from within, due to being fully pure from the Five Hindrances.

Continue meditating as before by stopping still at the center of the center of the Dhamma Sphere. Stop still and wait. When the concentration is just right, sphere after sphere pops up by itself from the center, each one inside the previous one. First comes the Sphere of *Sīla* or moral behavior, followed by the Sphere of *Samādhi* or concentration, and then the Sphere of *Paññā* or Wisdom. These are followed by the Sphere of *Vimutti* or transcendence, and then the Sphere of *Vimutti-ñāṇatassana* or the view of reality from transcendence. We call this, simply, the Sphere of Insight. Enter each sphere, successively, and focus your mind still at the pinpoint of bright light or hollow spot at the center. When the mind stops still, a new sphere emerges.

When you reach the Insight Sphere, you continue in the same way, stopping still at the center. Again the center expands itself. But, this time, instead of a new sphere, you see your own Refined Human Body, sitting cross-legged in meditation position, facing the same direction as you are facing. Don't be startled, just keep observing. It looks very much like yourself. It has your own face. But, it is brighter, purer, more radiant. It may even be crystal clear. Take your time. If you see the Refined Human Body, take your time to study it and get comfortable with it. Can you see that the figure is sitting on a thin circular pedestal? This is the *Jhāna* factors which support the body. Take your time to make the body and pedestal bright and clear.

When you feel comfortable with the Refined Human Body, place your mind gently inside the Refined Human Body. Expand to fill the whole body. Feel the body from the inside. Feel the arms. Feel the legs. Feel the head. Feel the toes. Say to yourself: "I am the Refined Human Body. I have become the Refined Human Body. I have the Refined Human mentality." Feel that.

When you feel comfortable inside the Refined Human Body, place your mind gently inside the sphere at the center of the refined human body. Focus on the pinpoint of bright light at the center of the center. The center expands itself. You see your Celestial Body. So Big, So Bright, So Beautiful. The Celestial Body is double the size of the Human Body. And, so much brighter. Adjust your mind's eye to the new brightness so that you can see clearly. Just take a moment of silence to enjoy the Celestial body. [Pause.]

When you feel comfortable with the Celestial Body, place your mind gently inside the Celestial Body. Expand, Expand, Expand, Expand to fill this whole big, bright, beautiful, body. Feel the body from the inside. Feel the arms. Feel the legs. Feel the head. Feel the toes. Say to yourself: "I am the Celestial Body. I have become the Celestial Body. I have the Celestial mentality." Feel that. Feel the bigness, the beauty, the brightness, the loving-kindness, the peace, and the compassion. Take a moment to enjoy that. Say to yourself: "I am the Celestial Body. I have become the Celestial Body. I have the Celestial mentality." [Brief pause.]

For those who reach this state of mind, go on with the same procedure. As larger and larger, more and more radiant bodies appear, become each more refined body, one-by-one, until you reach *Dhammakāya*. *Dhammakāya* looks like a transparent Buddha statue - very radiant! The Buddha statue, sitting cross-legged, is about 9 meters in height and width. Become *Dhammakāya* fully, right away. You will find this state of mind the purest and best happiness that you have ever experienced. [Brief pause.]

And now, let us share all of the merit that we have made in this meditation and previously - together with all of our loving-kindness - with all beings everywhere throughout the universe. We share with our parents, our grandparents, our family, our teachers and our friends. We share with our King and our Queen and the whole royal family. May Lord Buddha bless us all to lead a peaceful, happy life, free from suffering, free from problems and free from enmity. And may this meditation help to bring us closer to transcendence and Nirvana. [Pause.] And, now, we come slowly out of meditation and open the eyes.

Interviewer : Thank you very much, Dr. Phra Rajyanvisith. We reverently appreciate your exceptional meditation instruction.

Phra Rajyanvisith : May Lord Buddha bless you all. We would like to invite all of you to join us for meditation at Wat Luang Phor Sodh any Sunday. Our bus leaves from just outside the entrance of Wat Saket, the Golden Mountain Temple, at seven o'clock every Sunday morning. I lead morning chanting and meditation for all, beginning at nine thirty, and Phra Bart conducts an afternoon meditation session in English from twelve to two P.M. You are all very sincerely invited. Please come join us. For details, please see our English websites at ***www.meditationpark.org*** or ***www.dhammacenter.org*** or our Thai website at ***dhammakaya.org.***

Chapter 8
Summary and Conclusion

Summary

In summary, this is the second volume in a series presenting Dr. Phra Rajyanvisith's English-language Sunday Dhamma Talks on the National Broadcasting System of Thailand. It has covered the six months, from January to June of BE 2551 (CE 2008) and represents an extremely important compilation and explanation of Lord Buddha's most fundamental teachings on meditation, revealing the astounding depths and blissful heights attainable when Lord Buddha's teachings are properly understood and practiced.

The text began by completing coverage of the Three Higher Trainings *(Adhi-sikkhā)*, by adding Concentration Meditation (*Samādhi*) which eliminates the Five Hindrances through cultivation of the four *Jhāna* or states of internal absorption. This prepares the mind for effective *Anupassanā* and *Vipassanā* Insight Meditation. Chapter 4 added the Higher Training on Wisdom

(Adhipaññā-sikkhā), achieved through *Vipassanā* Meditation. The remainder of the book focuses on Four Foundations of Mindfulness Meditation.

Each broadcast also includes a brief meditation, encouraging listeners to "See for themselves." Thus, this volume both elucidates the teachings and encourages the practice of Lord Buddha's most fundamental meditation techniques, which can carry the meditator all the way to *Nibbāna*.

Dr. Phra Rajyanvisith's lectures have risen far beyond the ordinary in both scholastic erudition and meditation guidance. They have been filled with important revelations. His key lessons clarify Lord Buddha's teachings on meditation, correcting a handful of serious misconceptions and clarifying the overall picture. These insights are summarized below for your convenience.

Foundations of Mindfulness

The heart of this book expounds Lord Buddha's detailed teachings on meditation, presented in The "Greater Discourse on the Four Foundations of Mindfulness" *(Mahā Satipaṭṭhāna Sutta* of the *Dīgha Nikāya*). The sutta begins by stating the goal as purification of beings for overcoming sorrow, distress, pain and sadness, through gaining the right path for the realization of *Nibbāna*. Lord Buddha, then, summarizes the essence of the practice as follows. The meditator abides ardent, clearly aware and mindful, distanced from worldly craving and attachment, observing again and again body-in-body, sensations-in-sensations, mind-in-mind, and *Dhammā*-in-*Dhammā* .

Dr. Phra Rajyanvisith analyzes Lord Buddha's instructions into four steps: (1) ***Samadha* Concentration** into *Jhāna* to eliminate the Five Hindrances which distort our everyday consciousness; (2) **Human *Anupassanā*** contemplating the body, feelings, mind, and *Dhamma* of our Crude Human Being; (3) **Refined *Anupassanā*** rising through successively purer inner bodies, experiencing and contemplating the sensations, mind and *Dhamma* of each; and (4) Finally, ***Vipassanā* Right Wisdom** penetrating the Three Characteristics of Compound Phenomena, The Four Noble Truths, and The Eternal Truth of *Nibbāna*.

1. *Samadha* Concentration

Lord Buddha does not expound on *Samadha* Concentration in the Four Foundations of Mindfulness Sutta, but it is the necessary preliminary step to develop the inner peace and calm concentration to overcome the Five Hindrances *(Nivaraṇa)* which distort ordinary human thinking and enter the deep states of internal absorption called *Jhāna*.

The Five *Rūpa Jhāna* factors of Applied Thought *(Vitaka)*, Sustained Thought *(Vicāra)*, Joy *(Pīti)*, Peaceful Happiness *(Sukha)*, and One-pointed Equanimity *(Ekaggatā)* overcome the corresponding Five Hindrances of Drowsiness *(Thīna-middha)*, Doubt *(Vicikicchā)*, Ill Will *(Byāpāda)*, Restlessness *(Uddhacca-kukkucca)*, and Sensual Desire *(Kāmachanda)*.

There are four *Rūpa Jhānas*. In the First *Jhāna*, all five *Jhāna* Factors are already present, suppressing their counterpart Hindrances. As the meditator attains deeper and deeper states of ab-sorption, successive factors drop out of active con-sciousness. In the Second *Jhāna*, both Applied and Sustained Thought drop out. In the Third *Jhāna*, Joy also drops out. Finally, in the Fourth *Jhāna* even Peaceful Happiness drops out, leaving consciousness with only One-pointed Equanimity.

2. Human *Anupassanā*

Anupassanā means internal observation aimed at clear comprehension of the "Three Universal Characteristics" of this world's compound phenomena - Impermanence, Suffering, and Non-self. Meditation continues by focusing on the body, sensations, mind and *Dhamma* of our own normal Human Psycho-physical organism *(Namarūpa)*.

Mindfulness of the Body includes Mindfulness of Breathing, Postures, and Actions, Contemplation on the Repulsiveness of Body Parts, Reflection on the body as just the Four Elements (Water, Earth, Fire, and Wind), and the Nine Charnel Ground Contemplations on dead bodies. Mindfulness of Sensations is awareness of whether one is experiencing pleasurable, painful or neutral feelings and whether the feeling is sensual or non-sensual. Mindfulness of Mind is awareness of lust, hate, distraction, mental delusion, mental development, concentration, and liberation.

Mindfulness of *Dhamma* includes awareness of the Five Hindrances *(Nivaraṇa)*, Mindfulness of the Five Aggregates of Grasping (*Khanda*), Mindfulness of the Six Internal and External Sense Bases *(Āyatana*) and any fetter that arises dependent on these two. Mindfulness of the Seven Factors of Enlightenment *(Bojanga)* is awareness of Mindfulness, Investigation, Energy, Delight, Tranquility, Concentration, and Equanimity.

Finally, the meditator contemplates the Four Noble Truths. knowing that the origin of suffering is sensual Craving bound up with lust, pleasure and delight, which gives rise to rebirth, and that Craving arises wherever pleasure and delight arise - at the six Internal and External Sense Bases. Cessation of Suffering is abandonment of craving. And, finally, The Eightfold Path is the practice leading to the Cessation of Suffering.

3. Refined *Anupassanā*

The third step in the meditation is to continue on to deeper comprehension of the Three Universal Characteristics of this world's Compound Phenomena - Impermanence, Suffering, and Non-self. This brings us to the phrase "Body-in-Body," at the very beginning of the Four Foundations of Mindfulness Sutta, which has led to so much confusion.

Body-in-Body

Lord Buddha opens the *Mahā Satipaṭṭhāna Sutta* with the instruction: "The monk dwells observing again and again Body-in-body *(Kāye Kāyānupassī viharati).*" The problem is that normally we see only our one outer body. This has led some scholars to treat the phrase as an idiom and render it with interpretations like "contemplating the body as body." Amazingly, however, the fact is that thousands of modern meditators have seen "Body-in-body" over and over again, using the mind's eye during meditation. Dr. Phra Rajyanvisith's major contribution in this work is reviving and explicating the original sense of the words, based on the teachings of Luang Phor Wat Paknam and his own meditation practice.

As astounding as the "Body-in-body" seems, however, it is only a meditation tool. Lord Buddha's *Anupassanā* aims at Right Wisdom for clear comprehension to penetrate the Three Characteristics of all the Compound Phenomena of this world - both inert and alive, like ourselves. Such insight requires letting go of the limited, small-minded "self" mentality that we have each created and opening up or transcending to our higher mentality buried deep inside.

The "Body-in-body" is only the visible component of the Five Aggregates. By seeing, entering and ***becoming*** more and more refined bodies, the meditator takes on their mentality and raises consciousness to purer and purer levels with more refined feelings, sensations, mental states and processes, and deeper comprehension of *Dhamma*. This is present-moment direct experience as well as ex-post contemplation. Step-by-step, meditators can attain the Dhamma Eye or *Dhamma-cakkhu*.

Dhamma-cakkhu

The immediate impact of Lord Buddha's *Dhamma-cakkappavattana-sutta* was that Kondañña attained the "Dhamma Eye" *(Dhamma-cakkhu)*, transcending to the Right Wisdom to comprehend the ephemeral, illusory, enchanting, deluding, frustrating and ultimately tormenting fantasies which constitute this world's Compound Phenomena - including our own Five Aggregates.

Opening the *Dhamma* Eye appears to have been one of Lord Buddha's objectives. We deduce this from the words *Dhammesu Cakkhuṃ* repeated three times in the refrain. Success proved that *Dhamma* could be comprehended and established the order of Buddhist monks. Lord Buddha continued to teach each of the other four disciples individually until all attained the *Dhamma* Eye, and then taught the *Anattalakkhana* Sutta, bringing all five to enlightenment.

"Dhamma Eye" is not one of the Five *Cakkhu* taught in *Buddha Dhamma*. The five are four worldly levels: Human *(Maṇsacakkhu)*, Angel *(Dibbacakkhu)*, Wisdom *(Pañña-cakkhu)*, and Universal *(Samantacakkhu)*, plus the highest enlightened vision of the Buddha Eye *(Buddhacakkhu)*. What, then, is the *Dhamma* Eye? Lord Buddha's own usage of the term in the *Dhammacakkappavattana-sutta* makes it clear that *Dhamma* Eye is **transcendence** beyond worldly vision, but not yet up to enlightenment.

Elsewhere, Lord Buddha details all Nine Supramundane phenomena *(Lokuttara Dhamma)* as the Four Paths and Four Fruits of the Noble Disciples *(Sotāpanna, Sakadāgāmi, Anāgāmī,* and *Arahant)* plus Nirvana *(Nibbāna)*.

Thus, *Dhamma* Eye **transcendence** seems to imply **Noble Disciple** mentality. This mentality is detailed more precisely in *Vijjā Dhammakāya.*

Vijjā Dhammakāya

Meditators can appreciate Lord Buddha's refined *Anupassanā* from the *Dhamma-cakkhu* perspective, but *Vijjā Dhammakāya* provides detailed guide-lines for successively observing and becoming each Body-in-body and experiencing the corresponding sensations, mental states and processes, and comprehension of *Dhamma.*

Beginning at the Crude Human Body, the meditator concentrates and stops still at the center of that body and each inner body that appears, successively becoming each more refined body. He or she encounters the Refined Human Body (First *Rūpa Jhāna*), Crude and Refined Celestial Bodies (Second *Rūpa Jhāna)*, Crude and Refined Form Brahman Bodies (Third *Rūpa Jhāna)*, and the Crude and Refined Formless Brahman Bodies (Fourth *Rūpa Jhāna)*.

Then, the meditator transcends to *Dhammakāya*, seeing clearly with the *Dhamma* Eye. There remain, however, the ten Fetters *(Sanyojana)* or most deeply embedded defilements still binding one to earth. The Fetters are (1) False Self Concept *(Sakkāyadiṭṭhi)*, (2) Doubt or Uncertainty *(Vicikicchā)*, (3) Useless Ritual

Practices *(Sīlabbataparāmāsa)*, (4) Sensual Lust *(Kāma-rāga)*, (5) Irritation or Repulsion (*Paṭigha*), (6) Attachment to Pure Form Realms (*Rūparāga*), (7) Attachment to Formless Realms *(Arūparāga)*, (8) Conceit or Pride *(Māna)*, (9) Restlessness or Distraction *(Uddhacca)*, and (10) Ignorance *(Avijjā)*.

The first *Dhammakāya* Bodies encountered are the Crude and Refine *Dhammakāya Gotrabhū* or "Noble State Wisdom" who are transcendent gate-keepers, but not yet Noble Disciples. Thereafter, progress in cutting fetters is measured by Noble Disciple States. The word "Noble" *(Ariya)* is used to mean transcendent.

The Noble Disciple *Dhammakāya* Bodies encountered are Crude and Refined *Sotāpana* or Stream-enterer who cuts Fetters 1-3, Crude and Refined *Sakadāgāmi* or Once-Returner who greatly reduces Fetters 4-5, Crude and Refined *Anāgāmi* or Non-returner who cuts Fetters 1-5, and Crude and Refined *Arahant* or *Dhammakāya* Saint who cuts Fetters 1-10, attaining enlightenment and *Nibbāna*.

In any *Dhammakāya* state, the meditator can view and visit *Nibbāna* briefly during meditation due to temporary suppression of defilements by the *Jhāna* Factors. This greatly enhances development of the Right Wisdom to penetrate to clear comprehension of the Three Characteristics of all Compound Phenomena by permitting comparison of the ephemeral hollowness of this world's illusions with the ultimate, eternal Truth of *Nibbāna*. This contrast provides relevant, reliable and valid data which are firm and undeniable.

4. *Vippassanā*

The fourth Foundation of Mindfulness is contemplation of *Dhamma*. Lord Buddha specifies reflection on five key *Dhamma:* (1) The Five Hindrances, (2) The Five Aggregates, (3) The Six Internal and External Sense Bases, (4) The Seven Factors of Enlightenment, and (5) The Four Noble Truths.

This is where becoming body-in-body to gain supra-mundane mental abilities and comprehension of *Dhamma* really pays off. Contemplation is carried out in supra-mundane *Ñāṇa* rather than mundane *Jhāna*. Advanced psychic powers permit perception beyond human capabilities. Penetrating to lucid comprehension of the *Dhamma* - the True Nature of Reality as perceived by Lord Buddha during enlightenment - has been our real ultimate goal all along. Climbing the ladder of refined bodies is just a meditation technique for raising our level of consciousness, step-by-step, to develop the ability to comprehend and internalize these lessons. We are finally down to our ultimate task of penetrating Lord Buddha's *Dhamma*. Ultimately, this means penetrating the Four Noble Truths.

The Four Noble Truths

Ultimate penetration of the Four Noble Truths is attained by contemplating them three times around in three supra-mundane *Ñāṇa*. First is the *Sacca Ñāṇa* to know each of the Four noble truths thoroughly. Second is the *Kicca Ñāṇa* to know what one is supposed to do about each. Finally, the third time around is the *Kata Ñāṇa* realizing that one has already completed this task. This is the *Gotrabhū Ñāṇa* introducing transcendence, but not yet to the Noble Disciple level. Finally, Dr. Phra Rajyanvisith's concluding revelation is that these Four Noble Truths are not just external teachings, they exist at the core of our own being and can be con-templated directly inside our own *Dhamma* Sphere or nucleus.

Conclusion

In conclusion, this volume has focused on Lord Buddha's fundamental instructions about how to meditate, presented in the *Mahā Satipaṭṭhāna Sutta.* Lord Buddha concludes the *Sutta* with the strongest possible endorsement. He calls the Four Foundations of Mindfulness the...

...one way to the purification of beings, for the overcoming of sorrow and distress, for the disappearance of pain and sadness, for the gaining of the Right Path, and for the realization of *Nibbāna*.

Lord Buddha accompanies this conclusion with an elaborate verbal technique for emphasizing the incredible and rapid potential benefits of this practice. He concludes that...

...Whoever should practice these Four Foundations of Mindfulness for ... just one week may expect one of two results: either Arahantship in this life or, if there should be some substrate left, the *Anāgāmī* (Non-returner) state.

In this volume, Dr. Phra Rajyanvisith has revived the original sense of Lord Buddha's teachings on the Four Foundations of Mindfulness, highlighting how deep inside meditation can draw the mind - observing and experiencing again and again the "Body-in-the-body," "Feelings-in-the-feelings," "Mind-in-the-mind," and "*Dhamma*-in-the-*Dhamma*."

The astounding essence of Lord Buddha's teachings is that we each have an inner progression of successively more refined bodies stretching from this coarse outer shell through the Celestial, Form Brahman, and Formless Brahman Bodies in the worldly plane to ascend the transcendent *Dhammakāya* slopes which begin with *Gotrabhū* and rise through Noble Disciple States to *Arahant* and Nirvana. This trail has now been successfully cleared and ascended by thousands of meditators worldwide. This constitutes Lord Buddha's "one way path to purification."

This work represents an exceptional union of academic and transcendental knowledge, rarely avail-able in English. Please take it to heart and put it into practice. The broadcast series continues. Volume Three is on the way. Talks are aired on the first Sunday of every month at 8:00 AM, Bangkok Time (GMT+7:00), over four frequencies of the Thai National Broadcasting System: FM 88, FM 95.5, FM 107, and AM 918. We hope you can join with us.

Soundtracks and transcripts of the broadcasts, as well as guided meditations, can be downloaded from Wat Luang Phor Sodh's English-language websites: *www.dhammacenter.org* and *www.meditationpark.org*. For any questions, please email *bmi@dhammacenter.org*.

Phra Khru Baitika Dr. Barton Yanathiro
Interviewer and Editor

Appendices

DR. PHRA RAJYANVISITH

Appendix A

THE AUTHOR : DR. PHRA RAJYANVISITH

Meditation Master, Buddhist Scholar & Educator

1. Abbot, Wat Luang Phor Sodh Dhammakāyārām (July 9, 1991)

2. President of the Executive Committee, National Coordination Center of Provincial Meditation Institutes of Thailand (Elected by the Directors of Provincial Meditation Institutes from throughout the country at a Seminar and Practicum organized by the National Buddhist Office 23-25 April 2008 at Wat Yanawa, Bangkok, Thailand and recognized by the Sangha Body)

3. Preceptor *(Upachaya* - Since January 31, 1996)

4. Director and Principal-Meditation Master, Wat Luang Phor Sodh Buddhist Meditation Institute (Since 2006) *An Associated Institution of the World Buddhist University*

5. Vice-chairman of the Administrative Committee, Mahachulalongkornrajavidyalaya University Region 15 Academic Services Center (November 19, 2007)

6. Director, Dhammakāya Buddhist Meditation Institute (1981)

7. Manager, Rajburi Provincial Pali Studies Center (Appointed by the Sangha Body, October 20, 1999)

8. Director, Rajburi Provincial Meditation Practice Center (Appointed by the Sangha Body, March 6, 2001.)

Mission

Dr. Phra Rajyanvisith's mission is to revitalize Buddhism, placing equal emphasis on scripture study and meditation practice. He is currently 80 years old and carrying out the work of three ordinary men, working around the clock. He has published over 70 books, 400 articles, and two journals. He makes monthly radio and weekly TV broadcasts nationwide and internationally in both Thai and English, and has recorded over 1000 Dhamma lectures. His efforts have achieved noteworthy success both in the national Dhamma and Pali examinations and in training over 1,500 senior monks as *Vipassanā* meditation teachers. Dr. Phra Rajyanvisith has studied and practiced Buddhist meditation since 1970. He has passed Nak Dhamma Ek & Pali Level 6, and has taught meditation since 1982. From 1986-1989, he taught Buddhism at 17 universities and temples throughout the United States.

Wat Luang Phor Sodh

Phra Rajyanvisith has been the Abbot of Wat Luang Phor Sodh, which he founded and built, since July 9, 1991. The Wat currently trains over 10,000 participants per year. It has been designated by the Sangha Body as both a Provincial Pali Studies Center (on October 20, 1999) and as a Provincial Meditation

Training Center (on March 6, 2001). At that time, less than 100 of the 35,000 temples in Thailand had achieved this honor. In 1998, he received the Royal Ecclesiastical Rank of Phra Bhavana Visutthikhun, and in 2004 the rank of Phra Rajyanvisith. He received his honorary doctorate in Buddhist Administration from Mahachulalongkornrajavidyalaya University in 2007. In 2008, he became National Coordinator of Provincial Meditation Institutes throughout Thailand.

Educator

The major focus of his work has been on education, with equal emphasis on academic study and meditation practice. Academically, his Rajburi Provincial Pali Studies Center prepares students for the National Dhamma and Pali Examinations *(Navaka*, Dhamma 3, 2, & 1, Pali grammar, and all Pali Levels 1-9). Regular classes are supplemented by special examination review sessions. The Center has achieved unprecedented success. In 2003, all five candidates for the highest (Level 9) examination passed, making national headlines. In January 2007, four out of nine Pali Level 9 candidates passed.

Dr. Phra Rajyanvisith has led Wat Luang Phor Sodh to become the Academic Services Center of Mahachulalongkornrajavidyalaya Monk's University for

Ecclesiastical Region 15 (four central provinces). The Wat offers courses at the pre-university and certification levels, as well as a BA program in Buddhist Studies, and an MA program in Wat Administration.

Meditation Master

For Meditation Education, Phra Rajyanvisith's continuing training programs have prepared over 1,500 monks to become teachers of *Vipassanā,* utilizing his three textbooks teaching *Samadha-Vipassanā* meditation based on the Four Foundations of Mindfulness. He has also conducted semi-annual meditation retreats (May 1-14 and December 1-14) since 1982. These intensive practice sessions in small groups include living in tents, and are currently attended by 600-800 participants - monks, novices and laity.

In early years, Phra Rajyanvisith took meditation on the road with "Mobile Meditation Units" teaching meditation in some provinces throughout Thailand. The temple currently conducts 3, 5, 7, or 10-day meditation-Dhamma workshops for thousands of participants from various lay groups (especially students and teachers, government officials, business personnel and senior monks) year-round, except during the rainy-season.

The Wat also conducts an annual three-week "Hot Season Novices Program" for roughly 300 boys. In addition, there is regular Sunday Dhamma Practice for laity, with a bus leaving Wat Saket in Bangkok at 07:00 and returning around 16:00 every week.

International Outreach

Phra Rajyanvisith achieves international outreach thru the Wat Luang Phor Sodh Buddhist Meditation Institute, an Associated Institution of the World Buddhist University, established in 2006. It conducts three 2-week meditation retreats (May 1-14, August 1-14, and December 1-14) and year-round personalized meditation guidance in English. It also produces radio programs, publishes books, and supports meditation online thru its websites *(www.dhammacenter.org and www.meditationpark.org),* all in English for international meditators.

Ordination

On March 6, 1986, Phra Rajyanvisith ordained at Wat Paknam with the name Sermchai Jayamanggalo, sponsored by Phra Ong Chao Somsawali (Phra Worarachathinatdamatu, mother of the royal grand-daughter). His Preceptor *(Upachaya)* was His Holiness Somdej Phra Buddhakosajarn, then Acting Supreme

Patriarch, assisted by His Holiness Somdej Phra Buddhajarn (the former Phra Phrom Kunaporn), Abbot of Wat Saket and currently Chairman of the acting Supreme Patriarch Committee, and His Holiness Somdej Phramaharajamankalajarn (the former Phra Dhampanyabodi), Abbot of Wat Paknam. His meditation master was the Venerable Phra Bhavana Kosol Thera, who is now Phra Rajbrahma thera, Deputy Abbot, Meditation Master, and Director of Meditation Affairs at Wat Paknam Basicharoen.

Pre-Ordination

Dr. Phra Rajyanvisith was born as Sermchai Polpattanaritdhi on March 6, 1929, in Nangrong District of Buriram Province. He earned an M.A. in Public Administration from Thammasart University in 1965, and worked as a Research Specialist in the Research Office of the United States Information Service until early retirement at age 57 to ordain as a monk. During this service, he pursued advanced studies at the Institute for Social Research of the University of Michigan, Ann Arbor, and in Washington, D.C. In Bangkok, he also served as a visiting lecturer on research and evaluation at various Thai universities, including Thammasart and Bangkok University.

Address

Dr. Phra Rajyanvisith,

Abbot Wat Luang Phor Sodh Dhammakāyārām
Bangpae-Damnoen Saduak Highway (Km 14)
Damnoen Saduak District, Rajburi Province 70130, Thailand

Tel: (+66) 032-745-180, ext. 111; Fax: 032-745-170

Email: info@dhammacenter.org

Websites:

www.dhammacenter.org,

www.meditationpark.org.

Appendix B

BIOGRAPHY OF THE VENERABLE CHAO KHUN PHRA MONGKOL-THEPMUNI

(Sodh Candasaro)

The Late Abbot of Wat Paknam Bhasicharoen

The master of the *Vijjā Dhammakāya* approach, the late Abbot of Wat Paknam, the Venerable Chao Khun Phra Mongkol-Thepmuni, is fondly known and revered throughout the land as Luang Phor Wat Paknam, or simply as "Luang Phor Yai," meaning senior father or meditation master.

Luang Phor was born October 10, 1884 (BE 2427) to a humble rice-merchant family of Supanburi Province as Sodh, the second child of Nai Ngern and Nang Sudjai Meekaewnoi. As was typical in those days, young Sodh received his education from the temples. At fourteen, when his father died, he became the chief breadwinner for the family. Successful as he was in rice trading, at age nineteen the compassionate young man resolved to become a monk *(bhikkhu)* for life.

Having made arrangements to ensure his mother's welfare, the young man entered monkhood three years later, in July 1906 (BE 2449). At the age of twenty-two, he was ordained as Candasaro Bhikkhu at Wat Songpeenong, near his home. Phra Ajahn Dee of Wat Pratusarn, Supanburi, was his main Preceptor.

The day after his ordination, Candasaro Bhikkhu began meditation practice and study of Pali scriptures in search of deeper and wider knowledge, he moved from Wat Songpeenong to Wat Bodhi (Wat Phra Chetupon Vimonmangkalaram) in Bangkok. There, he frequented the centers of meditation practice and Pali study.

Soon, Luang Phor was recognized by his teachers, Phra Khru Yanavirati (Po) of Wat Bodhi and Phra Ajahn Singha of Wat Lakorn Tham, as an accomplished meditation instructor.

During those early dry seasons, Luang Phor adopted *Dhutangavatra*, the Austere Practices for Purification such as wandering in solitude through the forest wilderness, staying in caves and practicing the *Dhamma* with piety.

After ten years, Luang Phor set aside his informal study of the Pali Scriptures, having reached sufficiency to read the *Mahā-Satipaṭṭhāna Sutta*. Thereafter he devoted himself totally to meditation practice.

Luang Phor spent the next Buddhist Lent at Wat Bang Khoo Vieng, on Bangkok Noi Canal, where his benefactor, Phra Ajahn Choom, was the abbot. There, at nightfall on the full-moon day of September, in his twelfth year as a Bhikkhu, Luang Phor prepared himself for meditation in the *uposatha*. He invoked illumination and guidance, and made a vow dedicating his life to Buddhism. Luang Phor vowed not to rise from his seat in front of the Buddha statue until he was permitted to attain some understanding of the *Dhamma* as discerned by the Buddha.

With his mind set and its components of vision, memory, thought and cognition all at rest at the center of his body, two "Anguli" (joints of the middle finger) above the navel, Luang Phor was able to penetrate the full depths of the *Dhamma* as it was revealed to and by the Buddha. That revelation of the Dhamma and ever more refined *Dhammakāyas* (Dhamma bodies) was so profound that it was only possible when the mind was at rest at the body's center. After lent, Luang Phor went to teach at Wat Bang Pla, where three monks and four laymen who followed his meditation procedure were also able to attain various degrees of insight. Thereafter, Luang Phor gradually became re-knowned throughout the land.

Somdej Phra Vanarat, Head of Bhasicharoen Sangha District, spotted Luang Phor's potential and requested him to assume the Abbotship of Wat Paknam Bhasicharoen. This was a neglected and deteriorating monastery erected five centuries earlier. Luang Phor wanted to decline this request, but he could not. With utmost patience and remarkable leadership, Luang Phor gradually rebuilt the monastery until it is today one of the largest and most important monasteries in the land. In 1949 (BE 2492), Luang Phor received the ecclesiastical rank of Phra Bhavana-Kosolthera. This was followed by the title Phra Mongkol-Rajmuni, and in 1957 (BE 2500) by the title Phra Mongkol-Thepmuni.

Vijjā Dhammakāya, the revelation of the *Dhamma* as attained by Luang Phor, was the heart of his teaching. His service to Buddhism can be seen from his regular routine:

- Meditating day and night with *Bhikkhus* and *Upāsikās* in different sessions.
- Leading *Bhikkhus* and *Sāmaṇeras* in the uposatha every morning and evening, paying homage to the *Triple Gems* and ending with a sermon.
- Teaching public meditation practice every Thursday at 2:00 pm.
- Delivering public sermons on holy days (*Uposatha* or *Wan Phra*) and Sundays.
- Supervising the Pali Institute.

Thus, Luang Phor devoted his time and effort almost exclusively to teaching meditation. His disciples multiplied into the thousands. It was not uncommon for revered *bhikkhus* in far corners of the country, who apparently never met Luang Phor, to know him well and to respect him as their mentor.

His decease at the age of 75, on February 3, 1959 (BE 2502) was just a pause for the immortal master. His life should serve to remind other mortals to pursue their own obligations to the *Noble Path* carefully. Luang Phor's teachings live on, manifesting the *Ultimate Righteous Truth*.

Written by Phra Bhavana-Kosolthera
Veera Ganuttamo (Now Phrarajbrahmathera)

Appendix C

Wat Luang Phor Sodh Dhammakāyārām

Recognized Excellence

- Rajburi: Provincial Meditation Institute & Provincial Pali Studies Center;
- Sangha Ecclesiastical Region 15 Academic Services Unit for Mahachulalongkornrajavidyalaya University (Covering four central provinces)
- National Coordination Center of Provincial Meditation Institutes of Thailand
- Wat Luang Phor Sodh Buddhist Meditation Institute, Associated Institution of the World Buddhist University

Overview

Wat Luang Phor Sodh's excellence has now been recognized at provincial, regional, national and international levels. The temple is named after the late Abbot of Wat Paknam Bhasicharoen, the Venerable Chao Khun Phra Mongkol-Thepmuni, affectionately known by his birth name as Luang Phor Sodh. In 1917, he rediscovered the *Vijjā Dhammakāya* meditation technique, integrating *Samadha* and *Vipas-*

Wat Luang Phor Sodh is one of the most beautiful temples in Thailand and one of the most quiet places for people to find inner peace.

sanā to reach internal states of transcendence, in accordance with the Four Foundations of Mindfulness. The meditation is effective for both those who seek to understand reality and the meaning of life and for those seeking inner purification. Wisdom and virtue develop hand-in-hand as one progresses beyond the distortions of the passions.

The Wat's objective is to revitalize Buddhism with equal emphasis on meditation practice and scripture study. It serves as a provincial center for both meditation and Pali studies, and as an educational center for both the World Buddhist University and the Mahachulalongkornrajavidyalaya University for monks. It trains over 10,000 participants per year. Meditation retreats were initiated in 1982 by the precursor of the wat, the Dhammakāya Buddhist Meditation Institute. The Wat was registered in 1991. The campus is a beautifully land-scaped 33-acre park, featuring a lake and rivers surrounded by grass and trees. Temple buildings are vividly white, to signify purity. There are generally about 100 monks and 60 novices in residence, joined continually by hundreds of short-term participants in the Wat's constant stream of varied educational programs.

The address is Wat Luang Phor Sodh Dhammakāyārām, Damnoen Saduak District, Rajburi Province 70130, Thailand. It is located at Km. 14 on the Bang Pae - Damnoen Saduak Highway, 94 km. southwest of Bangkok. The number 78 air-conditioned bus from the Southern Bus Terminal will drop you off at the gate. The Wat Telephone number is (+66) 032-253-632 (Thai only). For English, please see ***www.dhammacenter.org*** *or* ***www.meditation-park.org,*** or **email : bmi@dhammacenter.org** or call Phra Bart at (+66) 089-068-0521, Phra Bill at (+66) 086-364-8808 or Phra Nat at (+66) 087-686-4635, or fax (+66) 032-745-170. The Thai language website is ***www.dhammakaya.org.***

Programs

The Wat conducts numerous educational programs on meditation and scripture study in both Thai and English, as follows:

Programs in Thai

1. **Sunday Dhamma Practice :** Wat bus leaves Wat Saket, Bangkok, at 07:00 and returns about 16:00.

2. **Workshops :** 3, 5, 7, or 10-day meditation-Dhamma study workshops for various lay groups - students, teachers, government officials, state enterprise/private business personnel, etc., (year-round except during the rainy-season), train over 20,000 participants per year.

3. **Retreats :** Two semi-annual retreats for hundreds of laity and monks, May and December 1-14, since 1982.

4. **Vipassanā Teacher Training :** Two-week courses for meditation masters, May & Dec 15-28, have trained over 500 monks. By 2010 The Wat will plan to have six two-week courses. The Wat might have the ability to train over 1,500 monks a year.

5. **Mahachulalongkornrajavidyalaya University :** Pre-university studies for Monks in Region 15, BA in Buddhist Studies, MA in Buddhist Administration.

6. **Dhamma Studies School :** Three month preparation for National Dhamma Exams (Nakdhamma 3, 2, 1).

7. **Pali Studies School :** Three month preparation for national Pali exams in grammar and levels 1-9.

8. **Radio Broadcasts :** Lecture on Dhamma (Mostly) every 3rd Sunday of every other month at 08.00 - 08.30 AM. on National Broadcasting Station of Thailand; Own FM radio station plus weekly and monthly national and international Dhamma Talks in Thai.

9. **TV Broadcasts :** Every 1st. and 3rd Sunday of the month at 05:30 on Modern 9 TV; every morning at 05.00 - 06.00 AM. on D- Station.

10. **Publications :** Over 50 books, numerous pamphlets, and a monthly journal in Thai.

11. **Ordination for Monks :** Ordinations most Saturdays plus special group ordinations.

12. **Ordination for Novices :** Two-week "Hot Season" Novices Program.

13. **Special Ceremonies :** Four major Buddhist holidays plus Dhammakāya holidays plus special events.

14. **24-hour Meditation for World Peace** Continual advanced meditation in shifts around the clock. New Meditation Vihara in the lake now in service.

15. **Pilgrimage Center :** Now building Phra Maha Jetiya Somdej to display the Wat's exceptional collection of Buddha relics. (See Appendix F.)

16. **Center for making merit :** The wat is offering very sacred Buddha statues as "Thank you" for major donations for Jetiya construction, some donated by celestial beings.

17. **Website :** Dhamma & meditation in Thai on ***www.dhammakaya.org.***

Programs in English

1. **Meditation Guidance :** Year-round, semi-private meditation guidance in English, which has proved astoundingly effective. Come anytime and stay as long as you like.

2. **Retreats :** Three intensive retreats May 1-14, August 1-14, and December 1-14.

3. **Meditation Online :** Meditation guidance, Q&A interaction, forums, and downloadable meditations at ***www.meditationpark.org.***

4. **Website :** Buddhist Meditation Institute (An Associated Institution of the World Buddhist University) at ***www.dhammacenter.org***.

5. **Radio Broadcasts**: Monthly Dhamma Talks over National Broadcasting Service of Thailand - 08:00 on the first Sunday of each month on FM88, FM95.5, FM107, and AM918. Downloadable from websites and published every six months.

6. **Publications**:

1. Phra Rajyanvisith 1991, 1997 & 2009, <u>The Heart of Dhammakāya Meditation Vol 1,</u>

2. Dr. Phra Rajyanvisith, <u>Sunday Dhamma Talks Vol 1, 2550 (2007)</u> with successive volumes every 6 months.

3. Dr. Phra Rajyanvisith, <u>Sunday Dhamma Talks Vol 2, 2551 (2008)</u>.

4. Dr. Phra Rajyanvisith, Sunday Dhamma Talks Vol 3, 2551 (2008).

5. Potprecha Cholvijarn 2009, Nibbāna as Self or Not Self: Some Contemporary Thai Discussions, MA thesis University of Bristol.

6. Mae Chee Amphai Tansomboon 2009, The Buddha Dhamma Propagation of Phra Mongkol Thepmuni. MA Thesis Mahachulalongkornrajavidyalaya University (2nd Ed.)

7. See ***www.dhammacenter.org*** for up-to-date listing of additional publications.

Appendix D

PHRA MAHA JETIYA SOMDEJ

Wat Luang Phor Sodh's biggest and most important current project is constructing Phra Maha Jetiya Somdej to enshrine sacred Buddha relics, to pay reverence to Lord Buddha, and to prolong the life of Buddhism. The Jetiya is expected to become a major Buddhist pilgrimage site for paying reverence to sacred Buddhist relics.

The Wat has an extraordinary collection of Buddha relics. There are crystal replicas of all seven relics which escaped cremation - the four wisdom teeth, two collar bone pieces, and the forehead piece. The original relics are preserved elsewhere, so these crystal reproductions were materialized and donated by senior celestial beings. In addition, there are numerous genuine relics. These include 115 pearl-sized pieces of Lord Buddha's breast bone, about 20 very refined hairs of Lord Buddha and many long black hairs of Prince Siddhattha, as well as many smaller granular relics from Lord Buddha and some Arahant disciples.

The Architect's Model
Expected Completion Date 2011

A Sample of Buddha Relics at Wat Luang Phor Sodh

The relics are not yet on outside public display except on special days. The temple is currently receiving donations to build a very beautiful Jetiya, Phra Maha Jetiya Somdej, for displaying the relics. Construction is currently in phase II. The foundation is laid and the first floor under construction. There will be four floors. The ground floor will house the management offices and provide a place for 2,000 laity to meditate, conduct ceremonies, and hold general conferences. The second floor will be a large meditation hall for 2,000 monks. The third floor will be a museum of important Buddha statues. Finally, the fourth floor will display the Buddha relics.

The estimated ultimate cost, including decorations, is 450 million Baht. This is a unique opportunity for devotees worldwide to participate in one of the most sacred enterprises of modern Buddhism. The Jetiya is destined to preserve the faith and revitalize the faithful for centuries. His Holiness Somdej Phra Buddhacharn, Chairman of the Supreme Sangha Body, is Chairman of the Jetiya Fund Raising Committee. Donating to this magnificent cause is the most effective merit-making opportunity any of us will encounter in this lifetime.

To express gratitude for generous con-tributions, the temple is offering a variety of very sacred Buddha statues as "Thank You" gifts. Some were received in sacred ceremonies from eminent celestial beings. Others are very rare and extremely valuable antiques Also, the names of those who donate at least 100,000 baht will be engraved in the Jetiya.

There are three methods for making a donation:

1. Directly at Wat Luang Phor Sodh

2. By mailing a crossed check (two diagonal lines in the upper right hand corner) to Wat Luang Phor Sodh, specified for Jetiya construction; and

3. By bank transfer to either (3.1) Bangkok Bank Damnoen Saduak Branch Account 422-0-25469-4 for Wat Luang Phor Sodh Jetiya construction, or to (3.2) Siam Commercial Bank Damnoen Saduak Branch Account 540-2-18485-8 for Wat Luang Phor Sodh Jetiya construction. When donating by bank transfer, please fax the bank transfer receipt with a covering letter giving the name, address and fax number of the donor. The Wat fax number is (+66) 032-745-170.

Appendix E

WAT LUANG PHOR SODH
BUDDHIST MEDITATION INSTITUTE

An Associated Institution
of the World Buddhist University

Meditation

Wat Luang Phor Sodh Buddhist Meditation Institute, an Associated Institution of the World Buddhist University, teaches Concentration-Insight Meditation *(Samadha-Vipassanā)*, which has proved astoundingly effective. Meditation proceeds to successively higher levels by always focusing at the center of the center.

Of the 254 meditators from over 25 countries served through January 2009, essentially all found inner peace, half meditated to trance absorption *(Jhāna)*, seeing their own Refined Human Body, almost four out of ten (38%) transcended to *Dhammakāya* or Noble Disciple level, and, more than two out of ten (22%) meditated all the way to the top, experiencing *Nirvana* temporarily. Most participants rated the experience very or extremely valuable. For some, it opened new worlds. Here are a few of the many tributes from former meditators:

- A once in a lifetime opportunity!
- Showed me a new world!
- Put life in a much bigger perspective!
- Encouraged me to live in a more altruistic way!
- In Nirvāna I was overwhelmed; I knew I don't have to doubt any more!

Meditation Guidance

BMI offers Meditation Guidance or semi-private tutoring in English all year round, starting whenever you choose and lasting as long as you like. If you have the time, please try to come for 10 days to two weeks, for maximum payoff. It generally requires 5-7 days to develop the inner calm necessary for rapid progress. But, individuals vary greatly, so all are welcome for either longer or briefer periods.

The program has many options, so each meditator can adapt it to his or her own preferences. Breakfast is at 06:30 and lunch at 11:00. We practice 8 precepts, which implies no eating after noon. The core of each day is either three or four guided, sitting meditation sessions, depending on how long one can stay. Meditations average 45 minutes. They are usually intimate, with not more than 5-10 participants. Meditations are recorded on MP3 for individual practice, and provided on CD to take home (Group A at 07:00, 09:00, 01:00, & 03:00. Group B at 08:00, 10:00, 14:00 and 16:00.) Serious Buddhists often add Morning or Evening Chanting and Meditation, held everyday at 05:30 and 19:00. Even casual visitors enjoy attending once as a memorable experience. At Evening Chanting, meditators can be taught personally, in English, by the revered Meditation Master, Dr. Phra Rajyanvisith.

Other memorable experiences include going along on the morning alms round at 6:00 AM and practical "how to live a good life" discussions with Phra Bill or Phra Nat. For those who volunteer to teach, perhaps most memorable are the fun interactions with monks and novices eager to learn and practice English (Daily 12:30-14:00). Participants interested in learning more about Buddhism can do this through directed readings and discussion. Finally, Most unforgettable for those who can scale the heights, is the indelible experience of the most lovely, most serene state ever experienced Nirvana.

The meditation atmosphere is the middle path – serious, but not overly harsh, with considerable flexibility in accordance with each participant's preferences. Meditators wear simple, white clothes to signify purity. Some white clothing is available free and top quality new outfits are available at the temple administration office for 490 or 990 Baht per set. Meditators take eight precepts – no killing, stealing, sex, improper speech, intoxicants, eating after noon, partying or entertainments or ornaments or makeup, and no high or luxurious beds. Sleeping is generally on thin mattresses on the floor under mosquito nets. Tents are available for those seeking more seclusion. There is no smoking on the Wat campus.

On the other hand, we do not practice "Noble Silence" (no talking), the food is the delicious (and often spicy) Thai cuisine that has become world renowned, and we have our own water purification plant. Vegetarians are generally asked to select what they can eat from what is offered, but the kitchen will do their best to accommodate individual requirements. Please know that they often cook for 1,000 people per day, so they are limited in how much individual attention they can give you.

Meditation Retreats

BMI offers three intensive retreats per year, May 1-14, August 1-14, and December 1-14. Retreats are similar to guided meditation, but more intensive, with a sunrise meditation at 05:30. They usually involve 20-50 international meditators. Several hundred monks and laity attend the Thai retreat simultaneously in May and

December. During retreats there is more access to the venerable Meditation Master in joint Thai-English sessions. This is especially useful for those who become advanced. There is also more chance to study Buddhist practices, Vinaya, Dhamma and Chanting. The large number of participants necessarily implies less silence.

The BMI Team

The Abbot and Meditation Master, Chao Khun **Dr. Phra Rajyanvisith** directs the Institute and teaches advanced meditation. He is one of Thailand's most eminent Meditation Masters, Buddhist scholars, and Educators. Dr. Phra Rajyanvisith has led the Wat to become a widely recognized center of excellence in both meditation practice and Buddhist studies. It is now the Coordination Center of Provincial Meditation Institutes throughout Thailand and the Wat's Buddhist Meditation Institute is an Associated Institution of the World Buddhist University. The Abbot is fluent in English and will personally teach advanced meditators.

Phra Bart or Khru Baitika Dr. Barton Yanathiro, an American monk, heads the BMI management team and teaches introductory and intermediate meditation with notable success. He is a former professor and international development specialist, with a Ph.D. in Sociology & Social Psychology from Cornell University, who has been a monk since March 6th 2002. Phra Bart was a professor of research methodology and was impressed by the depths of what Lord Buddha learned just sitting under a tree. He has concluded that meditation is the best methodology for understanding reality and how to live profitably, and is eager to teach it to all who are interested, worldwide.

Phra Bill or Phra William Akapunyo, another American monk, heads "Meditation Online" on the ***www.meditationpark.org*** website. Phra Bill, born 1964, first became a monk at Wat Mongkol-Thepmuni in Philadelphia on June 25th 2007. After a brief time out to see Thailand, he ordained again at Wat Luang Phor Sodh on Nov 29th 2008. He previously spent 12 years in the Navy and owned a T-shirt printing store. Bill initially contacted Wat Mongkolthepmuni to learn Thai, an activity that continues today. He distinguished himself as hard-working, dependable, and sincere. At Wat Luang Phor Sodh, Bill has demonstrated prowess in teaching mindful living through friendly interactive conversation and in effective outreach, coming up with our slogan, "Inner peace is closer than you think!"

Phra Nat or Phra Natpakanan Kunanggalo is a Thai monk who studied and worked in the United states for six years. Phra Nat is spearheading Publications and website development. He developed both the

www.dhammacenter.org website for BMI and the ***www.meditationpark.org*** website for meditation online.

Phra Nat ordained as a monk at Wat Luang Phor Sodh for the second time on February 8th, 2009. He graduated from Bangkok University in Marketing in 1994, and then ordained for his first time to make merit for his father who had just passed away. He was a monk at Wat Luang Phor Sodh from 1994 to 2000, and then left to study abroad in the USA. He earned an MBA from Eastern Washington University in 2006.

Phra Nat says: I have been a Buddhist since birth, because my family was Buddhist, but I never studied Buddhism until I became a monk in 1994. I have learned that the teachings of Lord Buddha are not reserved for Buddhists; they are for everyone regardless of religion, race, and color. If you study, you will understand for yourself. Especially meditation can be a big benefit for everyone in everyday life. Furthermore, the Four Noble truths, the heart of Buddhism, are very profound wisdom about reality that one should study in depth. You can see for yourself.

The BMI Team is assisted by many Thai layperson volunteers. Khun Vishan coordinates a large number of volunteers who help during retreats, and Acharn Damrong, teaches advanced meditation in Thai and Mandarin Chinese during retreats or by special arrangement.

Contact

Please see our website ***www.dhammacenter.org***, where you can register online or **email** us at ***bmi@dhammacenter.org*** or call Phra Bart at (+66) 089-068-0521, Phra Bill at (+66) 086-364-8808 or Phra Nat at (+66) 087-686-4635, or fax (+66) 032-740-170. For meditation online, see ***www.meditationpark.org.***

Wat Luang Phor Sodh Dhammakāyārām is 2 hours southwest of Bangkok by **#78** air-conditioned bus, which leaves from the left-hand sidewalk outside the Southern Bus Terminal, every 20 minutes 06:00-19:00. **Do not look for the bus inside the station and Do Not Take Any Other Bus!!!** Look for the bus in stall #1 or by the large blue sign in English towards the back of the sidewalk which says "**No. 78 Damnoen Saduak, FLOATING MARKET**."

Bus fare is about 70 baht, paid on board. Tell the conductress to inform you when to get down at Wat Luang Phor Sodh. Remind her again after 1.5 hours. (They often forget.) If possible, text Phra Bart **(089-068-0521)** or Phra Bill **(086-364-8808)** or Phra Nat **(087-686-4635)** your name and departure time as you leave Bangkok. Please arrive at the Wat between 06:00 and 18:00; it is difficult to make contact after dark. (We invite you for Lunch at 11:00.)

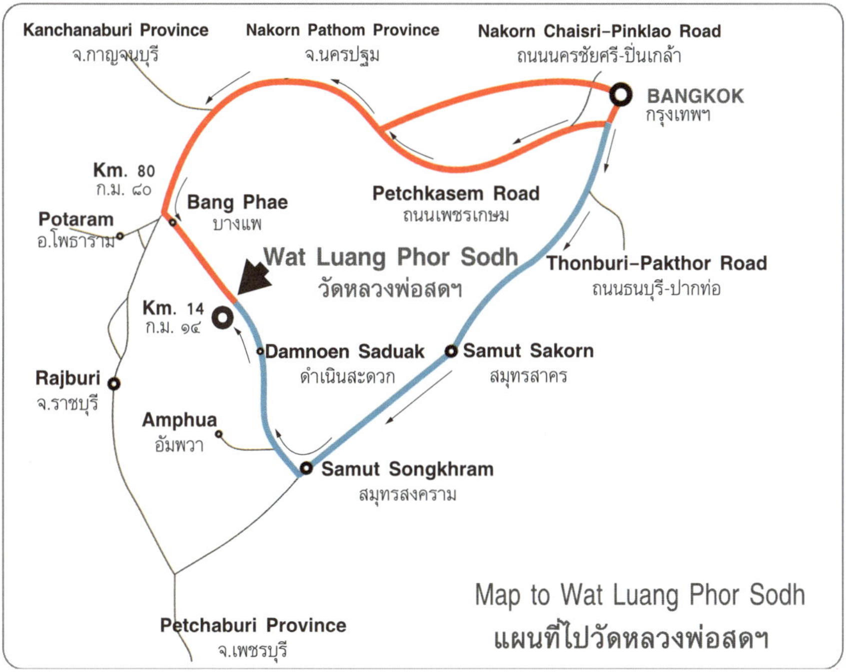

Map to Wat Luang Phor Sodh
แผนที่ไปวัดหลวงพ่อสดฯ

Map to Wat Luang Phor Sodh

Appendix F

WAT LUANG PHOR SODH WEBSITES

Wat Luang Phor Sodh has websites in both English and Thai. The English-language website is ***www.dhammacenter.org.*** Meditation Online is at ***www.meditationpark.org*** and the Thai-language website is ***www.dhammakaya.org.*** The English language website ***www.dhammacenter.org*** focuses on the Wat Luang Phor Sodh Buddhist Meditation Institute, an Associated Institution of the World Buddhist University, which conducts year-round meditation training in English. It also presents the abbot's monthly English-language radio broadcasts, which are downloadable as both sound-tracks and printed scripts. In addition, the website provides an ever increasing collection of original translations of key items of *Dhamma*.

The ***www.meditationpark.org*** website makes "meditation online" available to all who are interested, worldwide, regardless of geographical location, religion, ability to travel, or ability to pay. It is aimed at reaching out around the globe to those seeking release from the hectic stress of modern competitiveness or looking beyond the hollow emptiness of modern consumerism. It provides simple guidance to introductory meditation techniques which have proven exceptionally effective, together with direct Q&A interaction, forums, and downloadable guided meditations. Those who progress can advance step-by-step to gradually more advanced meditations. These are the same meditations that have opened new doors for meditators visiting BMI. Very few of our students are Buddhist. Most claim "no religion." We teachers are Buddhists, but we are just teaching meditation. We ask you to "See for yourself."